SHORT-TERM GROUP COUNSELING

Ellis S. Grayson

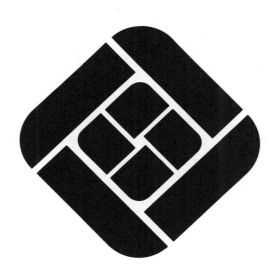

Perry M. Johnson, President
James A. Gondles, Jr., Executive Director
Linda H. Munday, Acting Director of Communications and Publications
Elizabeth Watts, Publications Managing Editor
Marianna Nunan, Project Editor
Jennifer A. Nichols, Production Editor
Cover design and illustrations by Ralph Butler

ISBN 0-929310-91-8

Printed in the United States of America by Kirby Lithographic
Company, Arlington, Va.

This publication may be ordered from:
American Correctional Association
8025 Laurel Lakes Court
Laurel, MD 20707-5075
1-800-825-BOOK

Contents

Foreword

Our evolving social structure brings with it difficult social problems that are changing the makeup of today's inmate and corrections' environment. In his third edition of *Short-term Group Counseling*, Ellis Grayson reaches beyond the sound, basic group counseling techniques he addressed in previous editions to tackle issues today's group counselor must address. New to this edition are counseling techniques for such current and vital issues as employment, stress, HIV and AIDS, drug and alcohol abuse, women's issues, and prerelease. Also new is a section on shared-interest counseling, which may be used to help reduce or end disputes between groups.

Short-term Group Counseling is especially geared to line staff in institutional or community-based settings who are called on to provide group counseling services in addition to their traditional duties. The value and appeal of this book lie not only in the practical and important information it provides but also in the casual and "readable" style with which the information is presented. *Short-term Group Counseling*, third edition, is evidence of ACA's commitment to provide corrections professionals up-to-date support and the tools necessary to work successfully in our changing corrections environment.

James A. Gondles, Jr.
Executive Director

Acknowledgments

I was very lucky. As a young man, I was employed by Dr. E. Preston Sharp, who was then the executive director of Philadelphia's Youth Study Center. (Later in his career Dr. Sharp served as executive director of the American Correctional Association). The center functioned as a detention and diagnostic residence for juvenile offenders who could not go home while awaiting disposition of their case. As group work program supervisor, one of my assignments was to develop an effective process of intensive and high-impact short-term group counseling, validate the process and methods, teach it to paraprofessional line staff, document the experience, and supervise its delivery. I did it, and this helped to start my career in corrections. I remain grateful for that opportunity.

In 1959, after two years' experience, I wrote a very skinny book titled *The Primer on Short-Term Group Counseling*. I wrote it for line staff, such as correctional officers and juvenile careworkers, rather than for clinical staff because I felt that line staff had more to give than was being asked or expected of them. My experience with line staff at the Youth Study Center, and the success many of them had in delivering group counseling to detainees, convinced me that they were an untapped source of service delivery well beyond their role, at that time, of watching detainees and locking doors.

There matters stood until 1978 when I accidentally ran into Anthony Travisono on 15th Street in Philadelphia, Pennsylvania. We had heard of each other, but we hadn't met until then. When he asked me to write an expanded up-to-date book on short-term group counseling, I jumped at the chance. Out of this came the 1978 publication *The Elements of Short-term Group Counseling*. Eleven years later, I was given the opportunity to update and revise this book. For these opportunities, I thank Anthony Travisono.

Now, under the administration of James A. Gondles, Jr., executive director of ACA, I was given the chance to further expand the book and produce a third edition. I marvel that my career has been helped by the kindness and support of people such as James Gondles, Ted Sharp, and Anthony Travisono. I am indebted to all of them.

When I look back at my career, which is still continuing, I recognize that I have been helped and supported by hundreds of my colleagues.

If I were to list all of them, this acknowledgment section would be as thick as a phone book. I remember each of you. Whenever I have young and bright people placed under my administration, I always remember that, when I was at their stage in the profession, a veteran helped me and gave me a great opportunity. So, I pass it on to the generations who have come after me.

It is in this spirit that I wrote this book, and others, for the field. It is my way of giving something back to the field that has given so much to me.

Ellis S. Grayson
Long Beach, New York

I. Introduction

Short-term group counseling is a time-intensive counseling process involving people in a group rather than individuals. It is a process where each session may be—but need not be—independent of previous or subsequent sessions. A participant need not go through a whole series of sessions to benefit. This means that each session must be well-planned and carried out to ensure maximum effectiveness.

By definition, short-term group counseling is time-limited. It does not go on forever. Unlike Moses, it cannot enjoy the luxury of wandering around for forty years before reaching the promised land of insight. As such, it tends to be directive rather than nondirective. It also tends to be goal-driven, that is, having an agenda of goals and objectives that must be specific, understandable, achievable, and measurable. Group counseling must address needs that have been targeted as critical.

Short-term Group Counseling and Corrections

Corrections must address a number of critical issues, according to circumstances, timeliness, emergent or potential crises, program and service needs, and future demands. New inmates/clients must be prepared to deal with their current predicaments and circumstances. Corrections must help them adjust to trying conditions where the cost of maladaptation may be severe. Corrections must also deal with the fact that the people it serves are often not easy to deal with and have not volunteered to be in their present circumstances. Many will resist or mistrust counselors or attempt to misuse their efforts and expressions of concern.

Corrections delivers services such as counseling not because the inmates/clients are who and what they are but because who and what corrections is. Corrections has a duty to the community, to the law, to society, and to itself to represent the best, wisest, and most competent—not the most uncaring, coldest, most repressive, and most damaging. Most corrections professionals are good, decent, and caring people. This does not mean that they are fools who open themselves to exploitation. It *does* mean that they have a responsibility to be competent and humane even in the face of frustration and provocation.

Treatment has been discredited recently to the point where a punishment approach has gained in popularity. It is important to remember that people are sent to prison *as* punishment, not *for* punishment. It is in this light and for these reasons that competent treatment in a secure setting is corrections' best posture. Treatment is not a substitute for security because the best treatment can take place only in a secure environment. No institution can deliver an effective treatment program if custody and security are so poorly carried out that the environment is chaotic. Treatment is vulnerable to a turbulent environment. Treatment demands an environment in which chaotic events and potentials are limited so as to avoid explosive volatility, which undermines treatment. Yet these controls should not go to the other extreme of being repressive because this also undermines treatment. Ineffectual treatment may provoke serious security problems, even in institutions staffed by a sizable security force.

Both security and treatment are everybody's responsibility in an institutional setting. The use of interdisciplinary teams and short-term group counseling provides corrections with opportunities for the coparticipation of treatment, custody/security, and education/training staff.

Short-term Group Counseling and Today's Inmate

The issues and concerns raised by participants in group counseling tend to mirror those of society. No institution or community can remain isolated from and unaffected by social currents. The pace of social change has been increasing. Individuals are given less and less time to understand, plan, and react. To be truly meaningful, group counseling must address contemporary issues and concerns. This may be done with grace and planning. It is really no help if counselors develop an understanding of the past but fail to understand the present.

This is a period of profound and rapid changes. The increase in the use of drugs with the attendant violence will certainly affect the thinking and behavior of individuals in group sessions. The job market has been escalating its demands for higher skills for entry-level jobs at a time when the Correctional Education Association reports 75 percent of the prison population is functionally illiterate. Corrections is charged with the task of preparing inmates with low literacy skills to enter or reenter the job market on their release. Unless work competencies and cognitive capacities are raised sufficiently, few of the jobs they are able to obtain will be attractive or satisfying.

Corrections is also becoming more and more sensitive to the needs of special groups. These include older inmates, the learning disabled, the mentally retarded, the mentally ill, and the physically handicapped. The decision to open and conduct a special needs group counseling

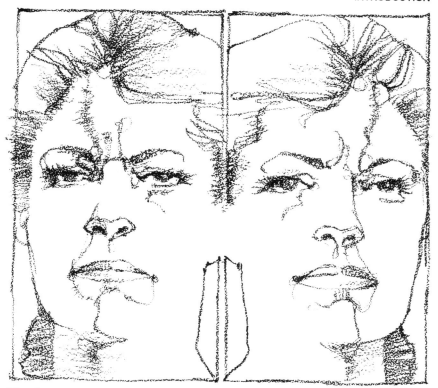

The issues and concerns raised by participants in group counseling tend to mirror those of society.

program should be based on the number who need it, availability of resources to carry it out, and capacity to deliver the services.

Women's issues and concerns present yet another area in which group counseling processes may be effective. Although there are myriad issues that are not gender-specific and that could be applied universally, there are many other issues that *are* gender-related. Such group sessions should, however, be led by someone who is open and sensitive to the nuances of women's issues.

Applications of group counseling are almost unlimited. In institutions, group counseling may be used for orientation of new inmates, for support to those who have problems coping with the stress of being institutionalized, as an adjunct to diagnosis and classification, for prefurlough or prerelease groups, for values clarification, and as a negotiating tool. Each of these situations has many questions and concerns that could be profitably explored.

There are also applications to teaching people how to handle critical episodes of their daily life. These episodes are critical because how well or badly they are handled can spell success or disaster or resolution or the generation of an even more complex problem. For example, most job titles have a job description that lists its major tasks. Yet it is possible for an employee to perform all of these tasks very well and still fail because he or she couldn't handle one or more of the critical episodes that tend to recur on the job—perhaps an episode that required the use of diplomacy—that is never specifically mentioned in the job description. Each of us, on the job, at home, and in social activities, might be able to perform more effectively by gaining more insight and skill in dealing with the critical incidents that confront us.

Group counseling, in its educative, reeducative, and ego-supportive functions, can be a useful tool in dealing with some of these problems. It is in this spirit that *Short-term Group Counseling* is offered.

This book aims to provide a basic understanding of short-term group counseling, its uses and some of its applications. It provides guidelines on how to introduce the program, prepare staff, plan and carry out the session, and fine-tune and improve the program. It is intended to guide somewhat like a cookbook. It describes some of the ingredients that go into short-term group counseling just as a cookbook describes the ingredients and the processes that go into the making of a dish. In the final analysis, the quality of the dish is not determined by the book, but by the skill with which the cook blends the ingredients and applies the recipe. No two staff members will approach short-term group counseling in exactly the same way. The structure of short-term group counseling encourages ingenuity and creativity, and nowhere is this more apparent than in the selection of the counselor.

Who Can Be a Short-term Group Counselor?

In an institutional setting, there are special pressures, challenges, and frustrations. Staff are seen as the direct agents and representatives of the same society and system that inmates (clients, patients, students, etc.) feel is responsible for their incarceration. Their feelings of rage, frustration, grief, chagrin, and resentment find several outlets, the most conspicuous of which is that of "dumping" on staff. If left to run their own course, such relationships quickly become adversary in nature, certainly counterproductive, and sometimes even lethal.

Correctional officers, aides, careworkers, and other staff with similar roles are often underused and overlooked, except in times of crisis. Yet these staff have the greatest sustained contact with the inmate population. The sustained amount and intensity of inmate-staff contact places such staff in the position of having to bear the brunt of inmate resentment and attendant behavior. Regularly being where the action is may have its drawbacks, but it may also be an opportunity for positive, healthy intervention if staff are properly trained and encouraged to use what they have learned.

Group counseling processes and methods offer these staff the skills and tools to intervene in a potentially effective way. When these staff are trained and encouraged to act as session leaders for group counseling, an opportunity is presented to maximize the positive potential of group member contacts. This book was written with such staff in mind.

These staff may be found in institutional settings for both juveniles and adults. They may also be found in community-based service facilities, schools, hospitals, and social service agencies. The work of the technician and specialist is being increasingly augmented by the efforts of such staff. In these settings, this book can serve as a guide and a training resource. It is an indication of the advanced thinking of an institutional administration if the skills and duties of such line, custodial, security, and service staff are upgraded.

The problem with traditional job descriptions is that they not only list what the job holder is expected to do, but they also limit that expectation to what is listed. It is difficult to expand the role of correctional officers or careworkers when the traditional understanding of that role—and the deployment of such staff—is narrow. This is one of the reasons correctional officers, careworkers, and service staff have been underused as treatment resources. Indeed, in some circumstances, such staff have been placed in roles that undercut treatment to the detriment of all.

It is not uncommon to find staff titles misleading because positions might be filled by individuals who, although degree-holders, do not have the professional background implied by their job titles. These staff members, too, may be maximized by involving them as group session leaders, following selection and training.

There are many settings in which those holding degrees in areas other than counseling may be appointed as case counselors. Those with degrees in English, philosophy, liberal arts, and education, as well as former clergy or teachers, have drifted into counseling. These individuals are paraprofessionals, too, along with correctional officers, careworkers, and other similar line staff. In addition to exposing such staff to case counseling training, some may be excellent candidates for staff development in the area of group counseling.

In a correctional setting, treatment and security are interdependent. It is because of this interdependence that traditional job definitions may be seen as too confining, leading to the underuse of staff who have more to contribute than is being asked or permitted of them. Correctional officers and careworkers, for example, should be seen as

5

having a greater potential for service than as serving exclusively as control agents.

Although community-based facilities are quite different from institutional settings, they share with institutions the need to maximize the use and contribution of line staff and to expand their roles and relationships with clients. The need to upgrade staff while improving the quality of service delivery is no less important to a community-based service facility than to an institution. In community-based services, the same opportunities can and should exist for interdisciplinary team involvement and jointly held responsibilities for case and group management. The complexities of case and group management today make it unwise to have counselors go it alone if team management can be practiced.

Throughout the field, then, there exists the need to reevaluate how staff resources are used and to upgrade that use. It is not cost-effective and it is demoralizing to staff to have them perform services at a level below which they are capable. It is also unfair to the client, inmate, student, or detainee.

Group counseling need not be so complex and mysterious a process that only staff who hold several educational degrees can carry it out. In countless settings, staff not normally considered capable of treatment delivery have been successfully trained and used as leaders/enablers of effective group counseling sessions.

This book, then, is not primarily intended for professionals with several degrees. It is intended as a resource for the training, development, and deployment of correctional officers, careworkers, aides, and similar types of staff whose time has come to participate in and contribute directly to the treatment, education, and counseling of those who have been entrusted to their care or custody.

There are many administrative difficulties connected with initiating such a program, not the least of which are scheduling, membership and staff leadership, conflicting demands, and needs of other services, operations, and programs. If group sessions are of such low priority that almost anything can preempt them, group counseling will decline in status and importance in the eyes of group members, session leadership, and other staff. Therefore, administrators must determine where group counseling is on their list of priorities and should not waver from that decision by allowing lesser priorities to bump sessions that are scheduled or to reassign staff to tasks of lower priority.

At one level of priority, few if any additional staff may have to be hired because enough lower priorities for staff coverage can be rearranged to provide leeway for the program. At another level, additional staff may have to be deployed. This decision is an outgrowth of many variables, and most administrators can construct the equation that will produce the options and choices from which a selection may be made and the trade-offs weighed. This is true not only for determining staff coverage but also for other aspects such as scheduling, use of space, and logistics.

These should be considered before the program is implemented. In addition, a staff development and orientation program should be initiated prior to implementation, using this book as an aid to staff trainees. It is less effective to use this book by itself because trainees would benefit from the guidance of a competent instructor and also from insight shared by fellow trainees. An instructor may fill in some material, ideas, concepts, and methodologies not covered by this book. In-service training may be used to modify some of the concepts in the book so that they may be tailored to the unique circumstances in which they are to be applied. Once in-service training has been completed, the book may then be used as a reminder and resource.

If there has been little or no preparation, orientation, or development of staff, the program may well fail. If the relationships between group counseling and other services have not been clearly considered and delineated, the program may well fail. If the program is used in ways for which it is poorly suited, it may well fail.

Group counseling is a modest addition to other programs, services, and efforts, not a substitute for them. It may add to case management, but not substitute for it. It may add to the quality of security, but not substitute for it.

Corrections has its goals and objectives like any other profession. Its mission is often spelled out in the laws that have established it and given it its mandates. When used as it should be, the process of short-term group counseling provides correctional staff with an additional tool to achieve these goals and objectives, thereby making it possible to better carry out corrections' mission.

II. The Evolution of Group Counseling

The development of short-term group counseling is tied to the evolution of people as social beings. Probably the first social group formed by humans is the family. In prehistoric times, the head of the family would call the family together to talk over the family's needs, hopes, goals, problems, and methods of solution. Codes of social living, group living, individual and group responsibility, and moral conduct were developed. Families began to combine to form groups, tribes, and other associations leading to communities.

As families, groups, tribes, and communities became more complex, so did the problems. This gave rise to the need for specialists. When the gods could not be contacted and satisfied except by a person who knew the secret ways, a priestly specialist emerged. In a similar fashion, there emerged the hunting specialist, the warrior specialist, and so forth.

With the growth of complexities in society, there arose the need for specialists who helped individuals define and solve their problems, both as individuals and as members of the group. These specialists were legendary wise men, often tribal elders with a store of experience to draw on. There were also tribal historians who committed tribal and family history to memory and called on this memory of generations of experience to help guide those confronted by contemporary problems. Tradition became the mainstay.

Society ultimately developed to the point where tradition, although not obsolete as a basis for understanding and solving contemporary problems, was not enough. New understandings needed to be developed. The history of religion, philosophy, and social science reflects the struggle to develop these new understandings. The Old Testament prophets, Moses, Jesus, Matthew, Mark, Luke, John, Maimonides, Mohammed, Confucius, Aquinas, Spinoza, Freud, Buber, Tillich, and countless others have contributed to the depth of understanding. Society has reached the point where its processes for resolving problems are sometimes more complex and sophisticated than the original problem. Technicians in society deal with these complexities:

certified professional social workers, accredited and certified psychologists, and graduate theologians and clergy, to name a few.

Short-term group counseling, as practiced by correctional officers, careworkers, aides, and similar types of staff, is not intended to duplicate or imitate the depth to which highly trained technicians deal with troubled people. Rather, it is a process designed to duplicate, in some ways, the earlier and less complex processes of people meeting in small groups to share concerns; to explore common problems; to gain serviceable insight, knowledge, or understanding; and to share these with each other.

There are certain useful levels of human insight and understanding that can be achieved with the help of a paraprofessional who is properly trained, motivated, deployed, and supervised. That discipline is necessary wherever short-term group counseling is used if it is not to be a pale imitation of group therapy or a lip-service response to the needs of the client population.

When group counseling first came into its own, it was not unusual for it to be confused with group therapy—often to the great discomfiture of therapists. Group counseling was seen as the light beer, with therapy in the role of the real thing. That confusion still has not been totally resolved.

Group counseling shares with group therapy the fact that both may serve to educate people, to teach them ways to behave that they never knew before. Both help people to analyze their traditional behavioral responses and teach them more effective ways of reacting or responding. Both may provide ego support—what some would call moral support.

Therapy is different from group counseling in that it deals with the building blocks of personality and enters into reconstructing the personality. Group counseling involves some techniques group therapists would not use simply because these techniques may get in the way of reconstructing the building blocks of personality. Group counselors believe it is possible to help many people see that they are thinking and behaving in self-defeating ways. Group counselors also believe it is possible to help many people explore alternatives to self-crippling conduct without necessarily engaging them in reconstructive therapy. For those who cannot do so unless engaged in reconstructive processes, therapy certainly might be appropriate.

Why Group Discussion

Case records of many juveniles and adults served in corrections indicate a high incidence of deprivation. Nowhere is the effects of this deprivation more evident than in the quality of their relationships with others. In some cases, well-documented, extremely abusive experiences were commonly inflicted on these individuals by their parents, guardians, and neighbors. The brutality experienced leaves its mark. This is equally true of simple neglect and unconcern. Individuals who have been abused, particularly during their early years, may well exhibit signs of abuse that go beyond the physical. These individuals are found in corrections in numbers far greater than most would suspect.

The most frequently used counseling procedure is group discussion, where areas of interest or problems are verbally explored. It is not merely group discussion for its own sake, but an open forum in which group members learn to better use language as (1) a socially acceptable means of expression and development of ideas, (2) a search for resolution, (3) a sharing of concepts, feelings, and beliefs, (4) a venting of excess emotional tension, (5) an exploration and examination of self and others, and (6) a tool in total adjustment.

This is important for adults and juveniles who have run afoul of society. Many offenders are inexperienced and ineffective in verbally communicating with others. For many, the only experience they've had in communicating with others has been in an atmosphere where people didn't communicate at all or where aggressive repression, in the form of physical and emotional beatings, was the common means of communication. For many, the opportunity to communicate has never before existed. Many have never realized that there are others who are interested in what they have to say about themselves and how they feel. Many have never experienced the dignity of being accepted as a person.

It is, therefore, not surprising to find these people nurturing hostilities toward a world they believe is the source of their anguish. Individuals' insensitivity to the feelings of others comes as a direct result of their world being insensitive to them. If individuals become hostile, cruel, or uncaring, it is their way of defending against or combatting the possibility of additional pain. Discussion in group counseling demonstrates that individuals can achieve recognition, learn about themselves and others, experience the dignity and warmth of being accepted as a person, learn to accept others, learn how to better handle their feelings, and achieve their goals in a socially wholesome way.

Short-term group counseling will not compensate for a life of hurting others or being hurt by others; of deprivation, abuse, and poverty; and of having been discarded. In effect, short-term group counseling is *not* a cure-all. It will not help everyone, nor should it be expected to. Indeed, some degrees of impairment require the more intensive process of therapy. There are some who are so impaired that any known techniques offer only faint hope.

Some may question whether group members may be harmed by short-term group counseling when it is conducted by a paraprofessional leader. Group counseling deals with educative, reeducative, and ego-supportive goals and objectives. It does *not* deal with reconstructive procedures involving the basic and most intimate building blocks of human personality, as does therapy. As such, group counseling's potential for inflicting harm is substantially limited. These limitations are further increased by proper selection, screening, training, and supervision of group session leaders.

It is also important to carefully select potential group members so that those who have especially fragile ego defenses are identified and considered for this process only with caution. For the most part, such individuals are not too difficult to identify. This is why it is better to have a staff team participate in selecting potential group members from those who volunteer for the program.

Some offenders are classified as having a character disorder. They tend to imitate and simulate emotions and feelings. They have little or no capacity for empathy (e.g., projecting themselves into the shoes of others). Any sympathy they manifest is reserved for themselves, seldom, if ever, for others. Generally, they may be included in group counseling sessions alongside almost anyone. However, individuals with character disorders should not be included in group counseling if they also manifest impulsive and/or aggressive acting-out tendencies, because this combination is volatile and potentially disruptive even under ideal circumstances. Group counseling, especially short-term, is probably not the ideal process for such individuals.

When selecting group members, caution should also be used in deciding whether or not to include individuals with histories of substance abuse. These individuals should be included only if they have been detoxified and remain so. Medical, health, and safety issues take precedence. This is an example of how an administrator must develop priorities within the service system and, in the case of short-term group counseling, determine where it is placed in the service sequence offered.

Working with People in Groups

Group counseling is quite different from case counseling, which is the individualized one-to-one relationship between the counselor and the person being counseled. Dealing with a group is synonymous with dealing with a compound dynamic that flows in several directions and dimensions simultaneously. What happens in a group counseling session is more than just the sum of the dynamics of each group member's participation. There is a bonus effect that goes beyond the sum of the individual participants. The interaction among participants creates something that could not have existed if each participant had acted individually and in isolation from one another.

A group comprises individuals as well as subgroups. Each individual has his or her own needs and his or her own way of expressing those needs. Each also has his or her own way of seeking fulfillment. This is also true of subgroups. There are alliances and antagonisms, some temporary and some semipermanent. The group counselor must identify each of these elements and understand how and why they interact. Only then may the counselor get a handle on what is and is not taking place in the sessions or happening to and with each individual and each subgroup. The numbers and kinds of relationships that occur in group situations make group counseling dynamically different from case counseling. Someone who wishes to be a counselor but yearns for a static and controlled situation had best forget group counseling.

Working with people involves working in an ever-moving and ever-changing dimension. People are highly complex. Some people have a range of behavior that is very broad and varied. The range of behavior of others might be, by comparison, quite limited. This is why some people frequently recycle their responses and repeat their mistakes, while others do so less frequently or invent new variations.

As each person faces life's problems, each pressure, stimulus, and movement in both the internal and external environment causes him or her to react and respond in some way. Even a nonreaction is a reaction, paradoxically. By pointing out and focusing on the positive values of the relationships within the group, the counselor uses a highly effective tool with which he or she can, with the group's support, help group members learn from one another. By examining as a group past and current responses that have failed, caused damage, or aggravated the original problem, a reeducative influence may be established.

It has often been claimed that even with the best treatment and influences brought to bear, people cannot change—a criminal will

12

remain what he or she is. People, however, can and do change. Some people are less flexible or open than others or cannot handle change quite as quickly or as efficiently as others. When a person's ability and efficiency in making necessary adjustments to life are impaired to the point where he or she cannot adjust to the requirements of the society in which he or she lives (and in a way that is socially acceptable), that person needs help. This is not necessarily true of someone who is a nonconformist, but it is true of those who act out their anguish and rage through murder, assault, rape, theft, destruction of property, harm to self, or some other criminal and delinquent conduct.

Not to be exempted from this are status offenders—juveniles charged with an offense that, if committed by an adult, would not be considered an offense. There is cause for concern about what is provoking such conduct and what can be done to relieve the provocations. Such problems and needs can be handled in case counseling. Therefore, group counseling cannot and should not be seen as being capable of dealing with a special variety of problem that is not responsive to case counseling. Group counseling is another process that, when used in conjunction with case counseling and other helping techniques, provides yet another vehicle for delivering help to people who need it.

The economy of dealing with groups is highly attractive. Few agencies and institutions have enough staff to effectively sponsor and deliver an individualized case counseling program. There aren't enough trained professionals for this, nor is there sufficient money to hire them in numbers called for in a case counseling-based program if caseloads are to be kept realistic. By dealing with groups, each professional makes his or her time count for much more. Where efforts of these technicians are augmented by the participation of correctional officers, careworkers, aides, and others as group session leaders, the use of staff can be maximized significantly.

From Me to We

The processes for helping people develop are sometimes most effective when they move in stages, going from the simple to the increasingly complex. As a person's skills, insight, and self-confidence increase, so do his or her capacities for coping effectively. Group counseling can provide opportunities for an individual to progress from simple and less demanding group situations to those of increasing complexity that are more demanding. By learning how to transfer and apply skill and insight to successively more intricate group situations, the individual can move from the specific to the general and, by this process, begin to see applications to how he or she functions in society.

Of course, progress is not always linear, going forward in a straight line. Backsliding and deviational twists occur in development. Group sessions can be used to help members analyze failures, successes, deviations, discoveries, and insights so that they may learn from failures as well as successes. All experience becomes grist for the learning process.

In a wholesome and guided group situation, individuals can be helped to experience a facility for sharing in and identifying with problems of others in the group. One of the most important dividends of the group process is the establishment of the "we" feeling. It is this feeling that differentiates the group from a mass, a mob, or an aggregate. One of the goals of group counseling is to establish and nurture the growth of the "we" feeling, giving it a positive orientation.

Counselors should encourage the growth of a "we" feeling within the group and use it as a counseling tool. For example, group members who share the "we" feeling with each other tend to feel less threatened, less anxious, and less fearful because they draw a sense of strength from the support they give each other. When this happens, some of these group members may then find the courage to face themselves more openly, directly, and candidly than they might without the feeling of being supported by the group.

Street gangs, for example, frequently have a "we" feeling, as do other antisocial groups. People band together and identify with each other for various reasons and needs. Sometimes, even those most closely involved may not be aware of what these needs might be— their extent, their power, or their urgency. Very few people have that degree of self-awareness and awareness of the needs of others to be completely in touch with what motivates them or the people with whom they are interacting. As such, there is no guarantee that a group that has developed a "we" feeling has done so for healthy and socially positive reasons. Nowhere is this more true than among gangs involved in drug sales and distribution.

This is why it is important for counselors to know not only what has happened but also why. If all they know is that the group has developed a "we" feeling, but they don't know why or what needs are being served, they may make some poor judgments and do some unwise things.

This is why short-term group counselors sometimes need to be assertive and direct. If the group counseling program had no time limits and sessions followed one after the other indefinitely, the counselor could be nondirective (which does not mean the same thing as having no goals or objectives) and let matters take a more natural and leisurely course. One of the characteristics of short-term group counseling is that the counselor is highly active, assertive, and directive.

If, for example, a "we" feeling begins to develop in the group, and that feeling then forms the basis for some potentially pathological group conduct in which the "we" feeling supports each member's negative acting-out, the short-term group counselor will not use the nondirective approach of allowing the group to work it out in its own good time. Rather, the counselor will assertively call attention to what is happening and set limits to the range and variety of acting-out. This is one reason why, in short-term group counseling, it is important to establish some house rules with the

Group members who share the "we" feeling with each other tend to feel less threatened, less anxious, and less fearful.

group before sessions are initiated. This is part of the structured process called guided group experience.

Guided Group Experience

Detention facilities, training institutions, prisons, and penitentiaries have frequently been criticized for being finishing schools for the criminally or delinquently oriented. Popular wisdom holds that what a person doesn't know about crime before incarceration, he or she will learn during incarceration. There is some justification for this belief.

However, it is possible to reeducate and rechannel group (peer) influence to achieve constructive ends. There is significant positive potential in the population that can be identified, liberated, and then encouraged. One way to do this is through the use of guided group experience that takes place as a product of group counseling.

One objective of group counseling is to help the group examine its values and the values of its members. In this process, the group is encouraged to look at what has happened to them when they have acted out or translated their values into behavior. By connecting values with acts and acts with outcomes, they learn to connect effects with causes; they learn that how they think and what they do are related to what has been happening to them.

If this process is successful to any appreciable degree, group members can be helped to understand that some of their values, and their conduct based on these values, need to be changed if their lives are to change. When this begins to happen, group members begin to establish codes of conduct—standards—to which they hold themselves, each other, and also the counselor. Because this is a double-edged sword, the counselor can hold group members to the values and standards they have begun to espouse.

In this way, the group can be helped to develop standards and values that are positive, effective, and socially acceptable. Positive group and peer pressure can be generated on this foundation.

This can offset traditional negative peer influences found in institutional settings. Where threats and force are used as primary countermeasures by management, the repressive effects can control negative peer influences for a while. The problem lies in what can happen in the event such threats or force become weakened or are so distant as to not be able to deter. In successful group counseling, deterrence is built in by becoming a part of the values and standards that can guide the conduct of the participant even when no outside controlling threat is felt. Control tends to be healthier when a person exerts it on himself or herself as an outgrowth of positive values rather than when it is imposed on him or her by an authority who is seen as repressive and unsympathetic.

Through a process of reeducation within the group, individuals who know only negative ways to achieve their goals or express their feelings can soon learn that there are other more socially acceptable ways to get along in society. In this process, the group and the individuals within it complement and supplement each other in an atmosphere of acceptance, sharing, learning, and constructive reeducation fostered by the sponsoring agency or institution and carried out by the counselor.

The Counselor and the Counseling Environment

Group counseling is a group-shared experience to which the counselor brings wholesome maturity and experience. Counselors have faced many of the same problems group members are facing or have faced. Counselors may not have acted out their problems in the same way as did the group members or, if they did, were more circumspect. Counselors are likely to have struggled with the same emotions and impulses as have group members. As such, counselors can understand the impulses of group members to the degree that they can understand them in themselves. This is why adequate and competent supervision of counselors is important to the success of the program. Supervisors help counselors better understand themselves and their functions while they, in turn, help their groups gain insight.

All of this should be done in an atmosphere of acceptance, devoid of vindictiveness, moral preaching, and recrimination. This atmosphere neither begins nor ends with the counseling session. To be most effective, it must be part of the total environment of the agency, institution, or facility. All too often, a special atmosphere is constructed for counseling or other treatment processes. When this special atmosphere is divorced from the day-to-day climate, counseling and other treatment take on an unreal quality that either discredits them or undercuts their effectiveness. The total environment has to be as decent as that of the counseling sessions if they are to have maximum impact.

It is naive to try to operate such a program in an environment that, outside of the sessions, contradicts everything these sessions represent. This means that the entire setting must, if necessary, be reengineered to reduce repression, dehumanizing conditions, and depersonalization—and such efforts should not be limited exclusively to the counseling or treatment area. Acceptance of an individual does not imply acceptance or approval of what he or she has done. Rejection of an individual is inconsistent with the kind of relationships that need to be established if he or she is to gain the courage or the motivation to face himself or herself and to effect positive change.

In providing individuals opportunities to explore themselves, they are also provided with opportunities to explore the following questions:

1. Who am I?

2. What am I?

3. What have I done?

4. What is my world like?

5. What is expected of me?

6. What should I expect of myself?

7. Where do I go from here?

8. How should I get there?

Group members are not the only ones to go through this process. Counselors, as part of the group, are also provided an opportunity to explore themselves. Counselors do not occupy a privileged position in the group session. They, too, become fair game in this process. In this way, counselors get to know more about themselves and more about the group and the individuals who comprise it. The group gets to know a lot about the counselor, especially as a human being who is accepting and accessible.

Offenders and Society

Group counseling provides an opportunity for group members to obtain factual information free from the unevaluated, uninformed, and speculative misinformation that often runs through agencies, institutions, and facilities. Some group members, perhaps for the first time in their lives, are given an opportunity to explore and learn about the values and standards emerging from a wholesome social relationship and to contrast this with what happens in street society.

The importance of such a process cannot be overemphasized. It is common to find group members who have run afoul of the law because of a clash of loyalties, standards, and moral practices between their immediate community and those of the overall society. To claim that an offender is antisocial is not sufficiently descriptive. Frequently, the offender does belong to a society, but it is a society with unique codes and practices to which he or she adheres.

Offenders often conform to a society as they see it, in which they claim "there is no such thing as an honest man" or "the difference between me and them is I got caught and they didn't," or if "they" got caught, "they got off and I didn't." Unfortunately, there have been many well-publicized events that even the most unintelligent offender can use to bolster such a view—and not entirely without justification.

It is not unusual for offenders to conform to the picture they have of an unjust and repressive society in which neither they nor their peers enjoy any real power except that which is temporarily generated by

An individual's concept of society is molded by his or her experiences in society.

their law-breaking conduct: a momentary high or an anguished act of rage that could not be repressed any longer. Many offenders come from neighborhoods where corruption flourishes and the need to survive, no matter what must be done, transcends most other considerations. In light of this, their wholesome experiences in group counseling settings can become of utmost importance to their rehabilitation.

It is wrong to suggest, however, that everyone who comes from poverty, deprivation, or an unwholesome neighborhood will necessarily become an offender. Even in the worst neighborhoods, the worst families, the most substandard living conditions, there emerge many fine and upstanding people. That so many escape to lead responsible lives is no reason to advocate the perpetuation of conditions of poverty, deprivation, and abuse.

It is important, however, to recognize that in deprived neighborhoods there are forces that tend to encourage, support, and reinforce delinquent and criminal behavior. For example, young people in a neighborhood with a high unemployment rate can see the pimp, the numbers runner, or the drug dealer living well and enjoying high status. They can also see the failure rates of those who tried it "society's way" and got their high school diplomas only to confront barrier after barrier that drained their hope and energy. They get a message from this, and some carry that message with them into jails, prisons, institutions, facilities, and agencies.

An individual's concept of society is molded by his or her experiences in society. Most offenders have had experiences that have warped their views of society. Some people claim that reality is in the eye of the beholder: truth is what is experienced and what is believed to be. Reality and truth, as perceived by offenders based on their experiences and needs, can be bitter and doom them to a lifetime of rebellion. Rebellion, by itself, need not be inappropriate. If so the American Revolution was wrong. However, how one acts out one's grievances and rages can spell the difference between those whose conduct is constructive and those whose conduct is destructive—of self, of others, of property. Robbery, for example, is not a legitimate expression of rebellion against an unjust life.

Group counseling can provide the opportunity for critical and constructive self-evaluation and the chance to learn how to deal appropriately with an environment within which all offenders must either learn how to cope or fail again and again. Group members are exposed to the idea that there are other and better ways of life. If there are legitimate grievances against society, it is appropriate to engage in social and political activism to effect social change—and there are ways to pursue such strategies, as provided by the system itself. But, if individuals wish to continue to act out their grievances by felonious conduct, then they must be helped to see themselves as being yet another exploitative and destructive element. A major function of group counseling is to help group members examine these issues, identify and use wholesome responses to these issues, and learn to recognize and use the wholesome forces that exist and will work in their behalf.

III. What Can Short-term Group Counseling Do?

The evaluatory tools in group counseling do not have the mathematical exactness of an algebraic formula. Those who look for exact answers will be disappointed. When we ask what group counseling does, we are also asking what its accomplishments are.

In the field of corrections, one standard measure that keeps cropping up is recidivism, repeated offenses, and convictions. As the theory goes, if treatment is successful, the rate of recidivism should decrease. However, this is a simplified notion.

In education, there is a time lapse, sometimes large and sometimes small, between the time one learns something and the time it takes to apply this knowledge. This is just as true of insight achieved in the treatment process. An offender may well have gained productive insight but, while learning how to apply this insight, he or she may have fallen afoul of the law once again. The offender doesn't need more treatment to obtain insight. He or she needs the opportunity to learn how to apply what has been already learned and the motivation to want to apply these insights.

Group counseling processes use methods and techniques that can provide these kinds of opportunities. One technique involves setting up simulated situations where group members, acting in various roles, attempt to apply insight to resolving the simulated problems. Here, they get some practice in a protected setting, facing simulations of the real thing. If done well, this is not unlike the way airline pilots are trained on simulators that duplicate various problems and prepare them for the day when they may face the real thing.

Social and behavioral sciences do not have complete knowledge of how much individuals help themselves, if they do so at all. There is such a thing as spontaneous improvement—improvement that is produced by forces and potentials within individuals, irrespective of what is done to help them. The human mechanism has the ability to affect balances, harmonies, and self-improvements. All too often, there is too much concern with those forces that cause imbalance, pathology, illness, and unwholesome responses. In corrections, it is recognized that within the worst offender, there can be wholesome potentials that, if properly identified and developed, could affect rehabilitation. Reeducation may provide such opportunities.

Reeducation

Reeducation is a process in which individuals are helped to examine their way of thinking and acting. In a group counseling session in which reeducation is an objective, individuals are encouraged to evaluate themselves and how they handle problems, as well as how what they do or fail to do generates crises and further problems.

The next step is to brainstorm alternatives, which are then put to the test by trial—through simulations, role-playing, role-reversal, and other techniques. Some of these alternatives will prove to be no better, or may even be worse, than the traditional efforts that produced the problems confronted by group members up to now. Some alternatives, however, will prove to be attractive and potentially more effective (and, it is hoped, more socially and legally acceptable).

When this happens, group members are given several opportunities to apply these alternatives to problems simulated in sessions. During this procedure, group members critique each other's reactions and expressions. Interaction among group members is encouraged by the counselor to build on itself. This is not an entirely free process. Certain mutually agreed on ground rules should be previously established by the group. Within these guidelines and standards, members encourage one another to develop and try out some workable and socially acceptable alternative thinking and behavioral responses. In effect, group sessions can become a laboratory where failure does not carry the extreme price that a similar failure in society may.

Group counseling provides an atmosphere in which individuals' potentials can be discovered, explored, developed, and tested. In a way, group counseling gives these potentials a healthy shove forward, and after that, it helps support and reinforce them. Thus, group counseling provides an atmosphere that maximizes opportunities for each participant to help himself or herself and one another. Some members of the group will be helped, but it cannot be predicted which ones or by how much. The counselor is obligated to provide the opportunity and to encourage participants to use it, remembering that participants cannot be forced to do so.

A successful group counseling program depends, in part, on the counselor's ability to motivate participants to help themselves. Duress of any kind is unacceptable as a means of gaining and keeping participants.

The reeducative effect of group counseling is based on some sound psychological principles. Everyone has a series of characteristic and habitual ways of responding to his or her environment. The process of reeducation is one in which these characteristic responses are examined and evaluated in terms of social acceptability, efficiency, effectiveness, wholesomeness, and lawfulness. When these characteristic responses are deficient as measured by these criteria, the reeducative process tries to encourage the individual to substitute more appropriate responses or to modify existing ones.

Group counseling may accomplish this in several ways. One is through helping group members understand what they have been doing and the logical consequences of their behavior. This is called insight.

Another way group counseling works to reeducate is through the use of examples. This procedure is important because an individual's behavior is the logical outcome of what he or she is and what his or her experiences have been.

For example, group members may complain that they have been the occasional victims of crime in their community. When the counselor asks if these events were reported to police, the members may be aghast. They are likely to reply, "Go to them for help? Man, you're crazy." This reply is consistent with the group's experience at that point. If, in group counseling, members can experience the example of the counselor—a representative of authority who wishes to help, who is genuinely interested in and sensitive to their problems, and who is not vindictive or exploitative—they may begin to think about others in authority as being capable of acting as a resource to which they may turn for help. In effect, the counselor may become a bridge to other helping resources.

Things do not happen in a group counseling session on a one-two-three basis. Progress is seldom linear and in a forward direction. Examples must be constantly reinforced and supported. First, the individual gets the example. Then, he or she has to be motivated and encouraged to test it. This first attempt to test it may be weak and hesitant. If he or she is rebuffed or discouraged in any way, the reeducative process may fail. The individual's first tentative steps should be noticed and encouraged in group counseling, but not through an overly syrupy, patronizing, and falsely laudatory response from the counselor. Such a response can be just as repellent and counterproductive as no response at all.

Giving recognition to positive progress on the part of the group or the group member requires skill and tact. If positive responses are subject to reward, it won't take long before the group establishes a premium for it. It is not uncommon in group counseling for the group to learn to encourage, reward, and reinforce positive responses from its members. When this happens, group pressure can be used constructively, especially with group members whose need for conformity to the group is great. In this process, group and individual systems of moral, behavioral, and social values become reoriented.

The reeducative aspect of group counseling encourages the group to try to understand the underlying motives and needs that stimulate their responses. When these responses don't measure up, group members are encouraged to learn better ways.

Through open discussion, individuals soon learn that their problems are not unique, that others have faced and still face similar problems. By comparing, discussing, and sharing, the group supports and aids members who are seeking to help themselves get along better in society.

Group counseling sessions promote a free examination of what society, the family, the group, and the law expect of each person. In addition, individuals are helped to better understand what they expect of themselves. Short-term group counseling fosters critical examination of how these expectations have been met. The group is encouraged to make constructive plans for the future, whether tomorrow or next year. This is the reeducative aspect of short-term group counseling.

Support

Being placed under lock and key or any form of restraint can inflict an awesome blow to one's self-esteem. There are some typical behavioral cover-ups used to mask and screen the effects of this experience. Among these are a show of bravado, a seeming unconcern, a fatalistic acceptance of the inevitable, or even a burlesqued acting-out of a "prodigal returneth greeted by a joyous noise raised up among the multitude" effect.

Some react to restraint and incarceration with overt fear, anxiety, or even depression. Others convert these feelings into expressions of rage, while still others become resigned and almost compliantly passive. In any event, few are neutral about the experience. For most, it is a very stressful time, but some are more skilled in hiding this fact than others. Some are so skillful that they even convince themselves that

Being placed under any form of restraint can inflict an awesome blow to one's self-esteem.

their defensive postures are real. Reality can be so painful that a sham, however gross, is less painful to endure.

The general public, and even many veteran correctional employees, tends to view inmates as a hard and calloused group. In a physical sense, a callous is a protective hardening of skin covering an area that has been abraded, traumatized, or wounded. A psychological callous covers wounds, traumas, hurts, and painfully tender areas of feelings. Many inmates really seem to be callous, and some are. However, most with experience in the field will know about the phenomenon of fronting, where a false image is created, either deliberately or unconsciously, to hide the truth.

Many drivers have had the experience of receiving a traffic ticket from the police. If they recall their feelings at the time, they were probably angry, upset, and remorseful. Most likely their feelings were bruised, if not hurt, as were their pride and self-esteem. Despite or because of such feelings, some responded in ways in which they tried to repair the damage. Some put on a veneer of bravado, although they didn't feel very brave. Some tried to demonstrate that they didn't care, although they really did.

Some denied guilt and any wrongdoing, all the while knowing they really were guilty. Some blamed the system, the police, or whatever authority they believed conspired against them—the simple citizen caught in a trap set by a mindless and unfair system while so many of the more guilty escaped.

There are countless ways in which drivers could have reacted to receiving traffic tickets that, on the surface, would not have truly reflected their actual feelings at the time. However they reacted, this cannot be offered as proof that they were not bothered by the experience, no matter how skillfully they covered up or modified their feelings.

Compare this, then, with the reactions of those who have undergone an even more intense experience—incarceration—and some parallels become apparent. Many of those incarcerated have suffered traumatic blows to self-esteem, regardless of how much, how well, or how insistently they try to cover it up or refuse to admit either to themselves or to others how great the emotional blow really was.

There are certain exceptions to this, including individuals who have a character disorder or those with serious psychiatric illness. Group counseling is a process aimed at the vast majority and not at the clinically pathological for whom other procedures—perhaps therapy—might be more appropriate.

Group counseling can expose and explore the feelings of group members in an open atmosphere. Group counseling can also offer support to those participants who need it to help them handle or diminish the pain of their current predicament. Without this support, few participants would feel free enough to truly evaluate themselves and what they have done. Without support, group members may not be able to get past emotional barriers that can prevent them from understanding why society has gotten so upset with their criminal actions. In short, support is given to sufficiently free group participants from anxiety, fear, and threat so that they can find the courage to examine who they are and what they have done.

This cannot be accomplished in a repressive, suppressive, punitive, and vindictive atmosphere. Although such an atmosphere may produce at least a temporarily compliant population—duress in sufficient amounts can achieve this—it cannot produce an atmosphere in which treatment is nurtured and helped to be productive. A person who has to deal with fear, anxiety, and rage has little time or energy left with which to deal effectively with self-evaluation and insight. Most of his or her energy would be directed toward self-defense and survival, just as it would be back on the street. A correctional environment that is no less threatening than the street cannot hope to offer effective treatment.

In an accepting environment, individuals do not feel the need quite as often to defend themselves or to construct a posture designed either to help them ingratiate themselves or to help them survive threat. Again, it is important to underscore the idea that acceptance does not imply approval of what has been done. Acceptance is, rather, a regard for the person, the human being, no matter what he or she has done. Even though the person is accepted, his or her accountability and responsibility for what he or she has done has not been diminished. Acceptance is not a new posture with which to relate to those who have transgressed. Accepting the person while rejecting the transgression is as old as the ministry of Jesus Christ. Group counseling has merely borrowed that relationship and incorporated it into the session.

In group counseling, participants receive acceptance and support from the knowledge that others are interested in them. They also get support from the opportunity in counseling to get pent-up feelings off their chest. This is called venting. A chance to voice or explore real or imagined grievances in a nonpunishing situation tends to serve not only as a support but also as a safety valve. Excess emotional steam can be vented in counseling sessions in a socially acceptable fashion. The more ways in which such avenues are provided, the more possible it becomes to prevent an uncontrolled and explosive venting that would require disciplinary intervention and control procedures.

One of the greatest supportive aspects of group counseling is the positive recognition each group member may receive for even the slightest constructive contribution to the group or for the slightest step forward. The experience of receiving recognition for constructive participation will not be lost on the individual or the group. There are few supportive devices as effective as success and recognition.

In addition to receiving support from the accepting atmosphere of the session, the counselor and the group are also sources of support. However, participants may not know how to tap into or even use such resources. They may not even recognize them as resources. In the group sessions, each member must be provided evidence that the counselor and the group can be helpful resources and also be provided with guidelines on how such resources may and may not be used. Without such guidelines, even the best resources can be unrecognized or abused. Counselors should also know that failure to support and enforce these guidelines can produce negative results.

For example, suppose the group is induced to give its support, either openly or covertly, to a member who is acting out in a negative and counterproductive fashion. There are many reasons why group members may do this. They may be angry or frustrated themselves and may be deriving vicarious pleasure from the acting out of one of

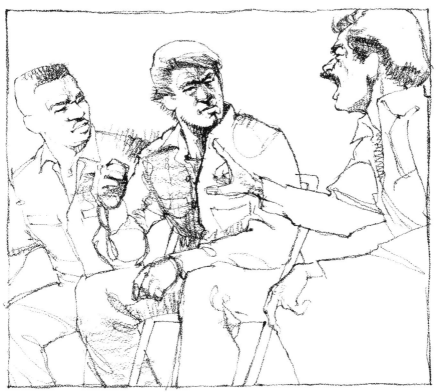

Excess emotional steam can be vented in counseling sessions in a socially acceptable fashion.

their number. Another possibility may be the counselor's failure to support and enforce previously established ground rules for the session.

An unguided group is no more predictable than an unguided missile. Who knows where or what it will hit and to what degree of destructiveness. With ground rules previously established and agreed on, it is possible to establish a rational process in which group members discover that each person can be a positive and supportive resource, and they learn that this is also true of the group as a whole. They must next learn how to use these resources in socially rational and effective fashions.

Group counseling can also be supportive when a member feels uneasy, anxious, or threatened, for whatever reason, by allowing the member to take refuge in the group. The individual can, if he or she chooses, melt into the group and not venture forth until he or she feels ready and secure. A good counselor will sense this and seek to provide the encouragement and warmth that will motivate the individual to venture forth and risk making a contribution to the group process.

It has been said that the typical offender, adult or juvenile, can be compared with the person who jumps off the top of a skyscraper and, halfway down, changes his or her mind. Group counseling helps participants realize that there are consequences that grow out of their behavior. Armed with this awareness, they learn how to predict what some of these consequences are likely to be. They also learn that if they don't like the predicted consequences, they had better change their behavior. Alternatives are developed, proposed, and examined as to likely consequences. This process also provides support because it builds greater confidence in the capacity to connect effects with causes, a necessary skill if one is to be ultimately able to avoid crisis-orientation as a way of life.

Group counseling processes can encourage wholesome forethought and afterthought, which can build the capacity for generating more effective, efficient, and socially acceptable responses. Participants are given a chance to try their wings in this respect, encouraged and aided by the counselor and the group. Through the group process, participants may learn how to organize and understand present and past experiences and how to apply this understanding to the resolution of problems. The goal is to help participants learn how to evaluate their traditional responses that have gotten them into trouble with the law, how to develop alternative responses for which they can predict a likely outcome, and how to choose the most effective alternative. As success builds on success, self-esteem will improve. As it does, participants will be in a better position to lend support to those group members who are still struggling and have not yet reached their level of achievement.

An Aid to Staff

A group counseling program can be an effective aid to staff. It may be used as a training device because its principles are applicable to every phase of corrections. By bettering one's counseling skills and knowledge, one can become a better worker irrespective of one's occupation in the criminal justice system. Even management can use these skills in their management of subordinate staff.

Group counseling sessions may act as a gauge of the group's feelings. Counselors may have a chance to spot difficulties before they become compounded or are translated into action. In a positive sense, it enables counselors to spot strong points in their relationships with group members and, by so doing, build and improve on these relationships. This can become an effective aid to disciplinary control as well as to program building.

Group counseling sessions tend to provide counselors information and insight on thoughts, feelings, needs, motives, and actions of individuals in the group. With such information and insight, counselors are better able to perform their duties. The methods, means of approach, program, and the execution of their duties will be effectively grounded in reality.

Group counseling tends to "humanize" the relationships between counselors and clients, inmates, residents, patients, students, etc. Through group members' participation in and contribution to group counseling sessions, they come to know the counselor as a human being and not just another disciplinarian, enforcer, lackey of the system, pig, hack, screw, or other authority figure. Likewise, the counselor can get to know the participants as human beings and not just another number, con, etc. The positive potential that can grow from staff and participants seeing each other as human beings is staggering in its implications. Beyond this, they can see each other not as adversaries but as people tied to each other in the same system. They are in the same boat and neither can sink the other without dire consequences to themselves.

Counselors can learn more about themselves. As a member of the group counseling session, the counselor is as open to achievement of insight and understanding as any other participant in the sessions. It is not unusual for counselors to get to know more about themselves through learning more about their needs, motives, aspirations, beliefs, and methods of response. Counselors may add to their own growth and maturity. This can lead to a more effective job performance and may carry over to their home and personal life.

This is an especially important point. Job stress in corrections has been recognized as significant. In some instances, correctional officers were discovered to have a heart attack rate more than several times greater than that of the general population. Other symptoms usually indicative of stress, such as alcoholism, family and marital problems, financial mismanagement, the John Wayne syndrome (a superaggressive challenging attitude with a penchant for violent solutions), and a lowered capacity for dealing with everyday frustrations, have been cited. Any program or system that can give participants the opportunity to obtain insight while, at the same time, offer the same opportunity to participating staff merits consideration.

Group counseling tends to bring together custody and clinical functions. In any agency, institution, facility, or human service center, one of the most regrettable situations is the artificial separation of staff according to their differing functions. In corrections, the split between custody and treatment staff is almost chronic and certainly wasteful. Most custody staff see themselves as career employees as opposed to treatment staff, who tend to have a far greater turnover rate. Custody staff tend to see treatment staff as naive, less than effective, and an intrusive nuisance. Treatment staff see themselves as overworked, underpaid, and unappreciated, but exemplary of humane concerns; the only bastion in an environment of goons and Neanderthals.

Noteworthy exceptions to this have been achieved by intensely dedicated and enlightened administrators. However, much remains to be done to reduce this problem of perception across the field. The close harmony that can result when group counselors bring together custody and clinical functions can improve the effectiveness of both custody and treatment operations.

Group counseling tends to enhance the professional atmosphere. Unless custody staff have some clinical/treatment role, they are too readily relegated to watchdog, turnkey, or nose-wiper roles that can be demoralizing and that certainly represents an underuse of staff potential. The professional atmosphere is improved when these individuals also function as counselors who contribute directly to the treatment process.

Group counseling can be used as a negotiating tool. There are times when correctional staff are called on to negotiate not with one person, but with a group. Sometimes this negotiation can involve dealing with an ongoing committee or an ad hoc grouping, either a representative body or one that is self-appointed. There are several sensitive questions and decisions that may need to be pondered before a course of action is undertaken.

If the group is essentially antiauthority and actively aggressive and contentious, it is difficult for any member who is vying for leadership and status with another or others to accept a compromise while in the group's presence without provoking a game of one-upmanship that quickly escalates. It may take a long, complex process to help the leaders come to consensus so that no one is vulnerable to any other's countermove of nullification or neutralization.

One strategy is to first negotiate to obtain a full list of claims, grievances, concerns, and needs from all who wish to contribute. Then, from this complete list, separate the issues that affect many from those that affect only a few. Once this is done, and the group accepts this division as valid, the next step is to negotiate an agreement on those issues that are most easily resolved. This helps to get them out of the way while establishing a sense that progress is being made. It is important for all participants to feel that they have gained something from the resolution, however slight that may be. Participants need to feel that what they have gained is at least of the same value and weight as what they have given up. Group counseling can help to convey this, thereby making it easier to pave the way for subsequent weightier agreements.

The following are some basic guidelines for using group counseling as a negotiating tool:

1. Time is usually not as important as sound process. Do not rush the process if doing so will create defects that will badly affect outcomes. Negotiators should make time work for them, not against them.

2. Review options with the core leadership, and especially review the likely outcomes—the downstream effects—that each choice is likely to produce. Try to get group members to figure this out for themselves—consequences as pointed out by negotiators may be seen and interpreted as threats. Do not make threats of any kind or say or do anything that could be interpreted as such.

3. Try to bring each issue to closure by helping the group

move to consensus on the issues and, following this, consensus on the agreements.

4. Do not, by word or action, suggest anything that would add to the list of demands, issues, concerns, and grievances advanced by the group. The negotiator's job is to reduce the list of issues that are keeping the factions apart, not to add to that list.

5. Suggest that individual issues that do not affect other people be handled by individual negotiation and, as such, be taken off the table. It is not unusual for one person to attempt to use the group for a private agenda. Try to get the group to support only those issues of general application and impact. However, should an individual's issue be of such a dramatic quality as to gain the sympathy of others, the negotiator may have no choice but to deal with it if failure to do so may arouse the antagonism of the group.

6. Make no promise or commitment that transcends the negotiator's authority or mission. If necessary, negotiators should call a recess so that they may consult with their staff team and their supervisors.

7. Use the technique of "active listening" in which negotiators fully perceive not only what is being said but also what may not have been said but is nevertheless implied. Ask the group for any clarification if needed.

When these few basic guidelines are followed, group counseling formats can become useful instruments of negotiation because the format does not need to involve the negotiator/counselor in adversarial positions, and it permits him or her to encourage personalization of relationships.

The many dividends of group counseling can be shared by everyone in the field: staff, participants, the agency or institution, and the community. Everyone shares in the responsibility for generating a wholesome community.

IV. Preparing for the Session

The early history of aviation is somewhat parallel to the early beginnings of counseling in that both offer examples of flying by the seat of your pants—a hit-or-miss intuitive approach. The number of individualistic pilots who did not survive that period in aviation far exceeds the number who were successful—and survived.

Fliers used to follow mottoes, such as "There are bold pilots and there are old pilots, but there are no old bold pilots," instead of sophisticated technical guidelines. From this beginning, one piece of technical knowledge was built on another until man walked on the moon.

Group counseling went from a fly-by-the-seat-of-your-pants approach to one that is characterized by planning, setting goals and objectives, and assessing sessions for some indication of the quality of the results. Of course, group counseling was never a life-or-death affair like aviation, but in both fields the days when one proceeded with faith and intuition, not planning, are over.

Planning is one of the first duties of the counselor who leads group counseling sessions. There are ways to plan ahead so that counselors can be reasonably sure of where they have been, where they are going, and how they may arrive at their goals. There are also ways to tell when one has arrived or if one has drifted, overshot, or undershot.

When counselors prepare for a session of group counseling, they follow much the same process as pilots who prepare a flight plan prior to take-off. The idea is to get where one wants to go as quickly and efficiently as the situation will allow, while planning for alternatives should contingencies arise. Therefore, what the counselor does before the session is of great importance to the successful operation of the session. What the counselor overlooks or fails to do might prove to be the root of failure.

What the Counselor Should Know about the Group

Counselors must prepare themselves with as much information on the group to be counseled as possible. This way, even seemingly insignificant bits of information can be of dramatic importance once the session is underway. Counselors who are fact-gathering before a session should not neglect information that pertains to the description of group members.

To a great extent, the session cannot be properly led or evaluated unless the counselor incorporates complete and specific information about the group into session plans. One cannot plan for an enigma. If counselors are to adequately plan and lead a group session, they must know the group in detail.

The following are some things counselors may wish to learn about group members before the sessions:

- age range of the group (e.g., juvenile, adult, young adult, senior citizen)
- interests, skills, and abilities of the group and individual members
- cultural, ethnic, racial, and religious backgrounds
- neighborhoods where members have lived and to which they are likely to return
- needs of individual members (needs they are consciously aware of or needs they may not have identified or may not even be aware of)
- varieties, types, and intensities of experiences members may share with each other as a group or among subgroups
- specialized experiences of some of the members
- histories of encounters with the criminal justice system (e.g., police, courts, probation, parole, institutions, etc.)
- sex (male, female, coed, including those who have significant problems with sexual identity)
- socioeconomic status
- educational levels and work history
- evidence of sociopathology or psychopathology in case records
- family histories, significant others
- history of medical/physical traumas

There are many other things counselors may wish to learn about the group prior to planning the sessions. As counselors gain more experience, their inventiveness will enable them to enlarge on their data-gathering skills, and they will expand on the database compiled, explored, and evaluated prior to planning the sessions.

Learning how to counsel effectively involves learning how to properly gather and organize information pertinent to the counseling situation. Counselors must develop skills to be able to recognize information that is important or potentially so and information that, however accurate, is not very important.

Statistics are helpful when in the hands of people who have good sense and honesty. In the hands of people who have personal axes to grind or hidden motives or people who do not understand statistics, statistics can be misinterpreted or misused.

The fact is that the correctional system is affected by the conditions in society that produced these numbers. The good and the bad of the community cannot be kept out of correctional facilities.

Statistics represent a composite picture of a group rather than a picture of any one person. Any given person in that group might be totally different from the group's picture. Statistics are often averages, with some people above the average, some at the average, and some below. For example, in statistics the situation of a person with one foot in a bucket of boiling water and the other foot encased in a block of ice may be computed so that the average suggests the person is comfortable.

It would be unwise to jump into counseling without having a good sense of the social, economic, and family conditions group members have experienced. It is also important for counselors to be sensitive to how such experiences can affect people.

Counselors should, additionally, have a good sense of what makes the group tick. The workings of a group are very much like the mechanism of a clock's wheels within wheels. The expression "group dynamics" means the way in which the group works. Few areas of information on the group are as important to the counselor as group dynamics. Counselors should, as much as possible, fully acquaint themselves with what makes the group tick before planning sessions. If they don't, plans for the session are not likely to be realistic or effective.

An understanding of group dynamics involves knowing the following:

1. Who are the group leaders? How do they lead?

2. Who is in rivalry with the leader(s)? How? Why?

3. Who follows whom? How? Why?

4. Who is left out of the group? How? Why?

5. What are the subgroups? Who belongs to each?

6. Who belongs to more than one subgroup?

7. What part do subgroups play in coloring the dynamics of the central group?

8. What are the roles of each group member in relation to the group and to each other?

9. What is each member trying to get out of the group experience?

10. Does the group change in behavior, goal, needs, and strategies?

These are just a few of the questions that can shed light on group dynamics.

What Shall We Talk About?

Once the group counselor gathers, sorts out, and figures out the content and patterns of data needed to plan the sessions, he or she is reasonably ready to evaluate potential topics for group discussion. The counselor evaluates potential discussion topics for meaningfulness to the group, timeliness, interest, need, appropriateness to the setting (e.g., institution, agency, community-based facility, etc.), and potential impact on the needs and problems of the group and its members.

What is meaningful to a group depends, to a great degree, on the past and present experiences of the group. This takes into account the needs, interests, abilities, and background of the group and the extent to which group members share these with each other. The speed at which the group can progress should also be considered.

The best topics to introduce are those that relate to the broad base of past experience of individual members of the group. Thus, each member of the group becomes a potential contributor. What is of little meaning to the group will have little affect on achieving the goals of counseling.

Despite the many things group members may have in common with each other, there may also exist vast differences. To ensure the topic has the greatest meaning for the greatest number of group members, the topic should be sufficiently generalized to permit each member the opportunity to develop meanings that can be shared by the group as well as be individually applied. A topic that is too specific may not be broadly applicable and sufficiently meaningful to many members of the group.

The counselor is responsible for selecting topics and matching them to needs. An alert counselor can frequently spot the needs of the group. Needs can be either long- or short-range. The counselor, in suggesting topics, does so with the goal of meeting needs that, at least for the moment, are urgent and pressing—even if the group's need is nothing more than the need to work off steam before going on to more productively rehabilitative areas.

The following are some highly generalized, broad-range topics that each group member can define for and apply to himself or herself:

- the future, the past, and the present
- success and failure
- the community
- the family
- friends—the group
- the present situation
- people in authority
- the law

These topics may open up several specific areas of application in the members' exploration of self, exploring such things as follows:

1. Who am I?
2. What am I?
3. What have I done?
4. What is my world like?
5. What are others like?
6. What is expected of me?
7. What should I expect of myself?
8. Where do I go from here?
9. How may I best get there?
10. What are my chances?

Questions and topics for discussion should be phrased to be highly provocative. Generally, people will not find topics interesting unless they are presented in a way to pique the imagination, convey a sense of urgency, and evoke imagery.

The topics, although generalized, should convey a sense of drama. Topics should convey timeliness, appropriateness, value, urgency, and meaning. Topics should be phrased so they are easily understood by group members. Complex words, obtuse allusions, and mixed metaphors should be avoided.

When initiating group discussion and exploration, the easiest place to start is often with the immediate situation and setting. The counselor, in his or her opening remarks, describes the what and why of the group counseling program. Frequently, a good session can be triggered by motivating group members to talk about what, if anything, they hope to gain from counseling. A productive session on this topic can set the tone and direction of future sessions and may frequently be used as a reference point for group members in gauging not only the direction of the counseling, but also how much progress they've made.

The counselor should select several topics and, from there, pick a few of the more dynamic for sessions with the group. The counselor should present the group with more than one topic to start the session, allowing the group to make a choice. The group should not be limited to one topic nor, for that matter, should the group be limited to the topics suggested by the counselor. Topics brought into the session should be thought of as suggestions for discussion, not as mandates.

The counselor is likely to soon discover that, although the group usually confines its discussions to the topics suggested, the group may have ideas of its own about what is of sufficient interest or importance. The counselor's list of suggested discussion topics serves to stimulate or provoke discussion—to prime the pump. If this process is poorly handled, it may limit or squelch choices on the part of group members.

In group counseling, the freedom of the group to choose also implies the freedom of the group not to choose. The counselor is not an absolute monarch, autocrat, or despot. Counselors must be careful not to conduct themselves in such a fashion no matter how worthy, pure, or benevolent their intentions may be.

What interests the counselor may not be of significant interest to the group. It is common for individuals to assume that if they are interested in something, then everyone else must be, too. After a few experiences in leading group sessions, counselors quickly learn that this is not always the case.

The story of Procrustes, a legendary giant of Greek mythology, helps to illustrate this point. Procrustes had a bed that he placed at the side of a road. He forced all those who passed by to lie down on the bed. If the passers-by were too tall for the bed, Procrustes amputated their legs. If they were too short for the bed, Procrustes stretched them on the rack until they were long enough to fit. From this story comes the term "Procrustean logic," which means to either stretch or cut down the facts until they fit preconceived ideas and wishes. Nothing could be more detrimental to the effective leadership of group counseling.

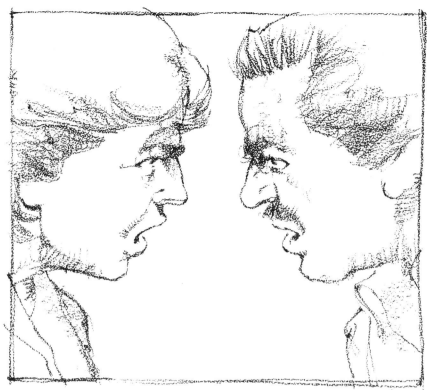

If the counselor selects a topic that cannot be resolved within the confines of the group, discussion will go around and around until fatigue or frustration sets in.

When selecting suggested topics for productive group discussion, counselors should avoid topics that cannot be resolved within the confines of the resources and realities confronting the group. Otherwise, discussion will go around and around until fatigue or frustration sets in. Some issues cannot be resolved because the requisite power, authority, knowledge, skill, or resources are not available. Counselors are not omnipotent; they cannot solve all problems. They cannot be everything to everyone. There are problems that are beyond them— and they should freely admit this, rather than make unrealistic promises and create expectations that will be frustrated in the end.

It may also be important to a counselor's sense of security in evaluating potential discussion topics to choose those that, by virtue of experience and training, he or she is familiar with and has competency

41

in. If the group discussion enters an area in which the counselor lacks sufficient skill, competence, or experience, it is wise to admit it. The counselor should hold off further discussion until he or she researches the issues or a resource person can be brought into the session. Another alternative is to suggest that the counselor and the group (as a whole or with interested group members) research the issues together and then reintroduce the subject in a subsequent session.

There are other possible strategies. Experience as a group counselor and good supervision can help increase the number and effectiveness of alternative strategies for handling problems. No one expects counselors to be experts at everything, nor should they expect it of themselves. In fact, even if counselors are expected to demonstrate expertise on a given issue, they should guard against the tendency to display this knowledge in a way that will intimidate or suppress the group.

The Importance of Communication

In a baseball game, a situation may arise where two outfielders stand motionless while a fly-ball drops between them. Each fielder thought the other was going to make the catch. At the other extreme, there are situations where outfielders collide because each believed he or she, not the other, was to make the catch. Both situations illustrate a failure to communicate.

Obviously, corrections is not immune from such failures to communicate. Corrections has its share of staff, services, programs, and operations that collide or, just as bad, wait for others to react until it is too late. The credibility of a group counseling program can be impaired if the program is carried out with ineffective communications. Even given the earnest desire of all staff to ensure the success of this program, it can be easily discredited by one too many botched-up episodes that could have been avoided had communications been better.

It is important for counselors to communicate with other staff who may have significant information about one or more group members. Information is useless unless and until it is shared by those who need it to carry out their function or to make vital decisions. How often has it happened that actions were taken or judgments made that were defective, ineffectual, or even potentially dangerous because a vital piece of information was either not available, not offered, not sought, not known to exist, or not used?

Group counselors should be part of the communications network so that they have ready access to sources of information and, just as important, are encouraged to contribute to these sources and to be seen and used as a source. In preparing for a session, counselors should consult with other staff and use their advice and information. When the session is completed, counselors should give these other staff some feedback, without violating confidentiality, so that they can see themselves being involved in the counseling process.

Communication involves sharing information on plans, procedures, methods, and results. In the final analysis, good communication among staff enables everyone to do his or her job better. It is part and parcel of the team approach. With proper communication, specialists, such as psychiatrists, psychologists, social workers, educators, physicians, trade instructors, and others, may be used as resources for counselors, groups, and individual group members.

With proper communication, the counselor may not only check the content planned for the group session but may also receive aid in understanding and evaluating the results. Input as well as output should be shared in such a way that the program is made more effective in its execution and is better integrated with other programs and services being delivered.

Another good reason for communicating is to avoid conflicts in schedules and priorities. Many people tend to think that what they do or represent is important. A group counselor is no exception. It is easy to become less than sensitive to other needs, services, and programs as one becomes more concerned with one's own mission and tasks. Group counseling can be perceived negatively by other staff if it is carried out in such a way, time, or schedule as to conflict with the needs and priorities of other services, programs, and efforts. It cannot ride roughshod as a pampered program without creating resentment that may ultimately reduce its effectiveness and credibility or actually expel it in time.

A group counseling session should not be scheduled to conflict with recreation, arts and crafts, shopwork, school, clinical services, and other activities. By scheduling ahead of time, the counselor will face fewer problems. The content and schedule will be made stronger through coordination, consultation, and communication. Once the counseling priority and schedule are established, however, it should be protected from incursions, cancellations, and co-options.

The Physical Set-up

Before the session, the counselor must arrange to reserve the room where the session is to be held. Just because a room has been used for previous sessions is no reason to believe it will always be available. Most rooms or meeting areas are multipurpose. It is wise to ensure availability to avoid conflict or embarrassment.

Counselors should ensure that the room is properly arranged as to seating, lighting, and temperature. One recommended seating arrangement is one in which participants can see each other. A circular or roundtable arrangement works well. The lighting should be bright enough for participants to see each other without strain and to see body language that is expressed, but not so bright as to be uncomfortable or intimidating. Temperature should be comfortable, but slightly on the cool side.

Counselors should see to it that any material or equipment they intend to use during the session is available and present in the room. This includes items such as chalk, blackboard, cassette recorder, video cassette recorder, television, etc. Counselors should have everything arranged and ready so that the session won't have to be interrupted to search for an item that had been misplaced.

In preparing for a session, counselors should consult with other staff and use their advice and information.

How the Group Prepares

The group should be given notice that a group session is planned. If the counselor has done a good job of preparing for the meetings, the group should already have been involved in the planning. Few of the group members, if any, are immune to the air of expectancy. To some members, the forthcoming session is something to be both anticipated and feared.

It is quite common for some group members to increasingly manifest displays of anxiety and tension. In anticipation, each member reacts in his or her own unique fashion as dictated by his or her personality structure. For some members, the upcoming session is like a fascinating and magnetic object that inexorably draws them closer while they experience an increasing sense of adventure and excitement. Some members are unbelieving. They plan to fully test the situation, the counselor, and the other participants before going much further. They have a diminished capacity and/or willingness to trust.

A few members may refrain from making some sort of plan on how to meet the counseling situation. Some make plans silently, to themselves. Others may band together to speculate on and plan for ways in which to deal with situations that may arise in the session. It is a rare member who doesn't dwell over the possibilities and make some plans, however tentative, to deal with the group counseling session and the counselor.

The following are some common kinds of defensive group planning:

1. Planning what to say or talk about. Many members derive a sense of security by planning ahead of time what they intend to talk about and also what they do not intend to talk about. Few members can stick to these plans once the session is underway. The impulse to speak up and react is frequently greater than the best-laid plans.

2. Planning to put the counselor on the spot. The plan is simple and generally works better when tried on a new counselor or one who is not self-disciplined. The plan might involve asking some embarrassing or provocative questions. The theory is that the best defense is a good offense. Counselors should not let this get out of hand.

   One approach is for the counselor to point out to group members what they are doing and to ask them why they feel they have to do it. This approach accomplishes a number of things. First, it tosses the ball back to the group. Second, it inhibits the group from verbally acting out beyond

45

a point they can handle without creating further distracting problems. Third, it tends to focus the group's attention on its behavior and the needs that trigger it. Last, it lets the group know that the counselor is alert to what's going on and is cool enough to handle it well.

3. Planning to remain affectless or silent during the session. The group plays a waiting game with the counselor. It is rare to find a group successful at this. Again, it tends to work better on new counselors or on those who are impatient or undisciplined. If the counselor is professional enough to control and understand his or her own anxieties and is able to wait out the situation in a relaxed fashion, the tension usually becomes almost unbearable and some members are driven by inner anxiety to break the silence.

4. Planning to control the session by (a) getting the counselor to talk about himself or herself, (b) planning to talk about "safe" things and tangents, steering the session to what they have reason to believe the counselor likes or wants to hear—an "amen" session, or (c) encouraging one of the more articulate members to gradually begin to assume some of the role of the counselor, e.g., leader/enabler.

Group planning, however defensive its orientation, is of great potential value. When the group is kept busy planning for the session, it has less time left for the kind of thinking and planning that creates disciplinary or management problems. More important, planning involves the exercise of forethought, which can be directed in positive channels by a skillful counselor. All too frequently, group members get into trouble because of a lack of positive forethought and planning. Impulsiveness is one of the great ingredients of crisis and defeat.

One of the most important positives of the group's planning is that it encourages the beginning of forethought. Initially, however, this effort may be no more positive than any of the rest of the group's conduct and, indeed, there is no reason to expect any difference. How well this may be redirected into more positive channels depends on the following things:

- the level of trust that builds between the group and the counselor
- the skill of the counselor in helping to generate some attitudinal changes among key group members

- the building of an increased awareness that group counseling can help them and is potentially valuable to them

- how well and genuinely the positive responses are recognized, encouraged, supported, and rewarded—not only by the counselor but by the group and others in the treatment environment (This is one reason why mutual support between staff and program services can be important to each other's success.)

In a way, group counseling can prime the pump by encouraging group members to think things through before taking action. Planning is evidence of forethought, but not necessarily positive forethought. Group counseling can help generate desirable positive channels of forethought and planning by the way the counselor handles these situations and uses them as elements to provoke examination, insight, and reeducation.

Planning should not imply a lack of truth or candor on the part of the group or its members. For example, there are many occasions when group members may purposefully lie about their desire to adhere to a straight lifestyle. They may be doing nothing more than playing for the acceptance of the counselor, especially if they have had success with this ploy in the past. In fact, there is really nothing wrong with seeking the approval of the counselor. It is only one of many responses, and it is in the significance of this response that the counselor invests interest. Very rarely is stating or implying that individuals are liars considered to be proper handling.

In effect, what group members start out believing is not quite as important as what they end up believing and doing. The response of the counselor is not to call members liars or to claim that they are "gaming," but to accept the fact that this conduct is a frequently used defense. One goal is to help individuals understand that they are accepted, that they are not under threat or attack, and as such, they don't need this defense: alternative ways of acting out the need for approval might be better. It is the function of the group process to help members recognize that they have this need and to understand why they have it. A purpose of group counseling is getting at and exploring the feelings and needs of the group and its individual members to promote insight, attitudinal change, and ultimately, behavioral change.

This illustrates the kind of philosophy counselors will find most productive in their efforts to counsel a group. Other things will happen in group sessions that will require the application of the same kind of philosophy. This philosophy, in brief, is: The counselor encourages responses and then helps the group to understand what triggered them. In this way, each member has the opportunity to learn more about what makes him or her and others tick and also what can be done to make behavior wholesome and effective. Squelch such responses and the process is squelched. This is why it is so important to establish an air of acceptance and support in the counseling session.

This doesn't mean that any and all responses should be accepted and permitted. There should be ground rules about limits, negotiated with the group and agreed to by all, such as no physically assaultive or threatening ways of acting out and no destruction of property as a means of acting out. Within set and agreed-on limits, the responses of the group and its members are grist for examination, discussion, analysis, and the provocation of insight.

After planning is completed, the counselor is ready to start the group counseling session.

V. Conducting the Session

The session begins with the gathering of the group. Observant counselors can learn much from group members' body language and verbal comments taking place at that time. The counselor can get clues from posture, gait, nervous mannerisms, who interacts with whom, attention-getting conduct, perspiration on the palms (determined by hand-shaking), where group members sit in relation to each other and to the counselor, and many other behavioral giveaways. It may be possible to pick out members who are more nervous than usual, a higher-than-usual level of agitation in the group, the existence of issues that may be more significant than those the counselor had planned to explore, or other considerations.

When group members gather in the room, the counselor may either seat them or encourage them to seat themselves. For diagnostic insight, it might be better to be nondirective and see where each person chooses to sit. The session can get interesting if, for example, one member takes the seat normally used by the counselor or by the acknowledged leader of the group.

Once everyone is seated, the counselor makes sure everyone knows each other, making necessary introductions or encouraging new members to introduce themselves. At this point, the counselor should be aware of any anxiety building up in the group. If the atmosphere gets a little too tense, a good joke works wonders to break tension. Relaxed informality should be encouraged.

First impressions often play an important role in determining the structure of future interactions. First impressions can be difficult to modify. Rather than having to go through a complex process of trying to squeeze the toothpaste back into the tube, it is much better to structure the situation so that the first impression is favorable or likely to be so.

Although it is a big mistake to make a poor impression, it is an even bigger and more costly mistake to create a false picture in the effort to make a good impression. Such false impressions cannot be maintained, especially in the face of the searching inquiries that characterize group counseling. Counselors should not embellish, dress-up, or overstate, but should be open, accurate, and unpretentious.

When introducing the session, the counselor should try to make group members as comfortable as the situation will allow. Using a little bit of humor, not at anyone's expense, can often break the ice. Retelling a pleasant incident or experience in which the group has shared is another method. Many of us have been to parties where various devices were used to build up social interaction among the guests. Many of these devices can be successfully applied to make group members comfortable in a group counseling setting. As counselors become more at home in group counseling, they will pick up several additional methods of easing counterproductive anxieties of the group.

It is important to lessen the anxiety group members bring to the session, because allowing them to heavily invest their energies in unnecessary defenses leaves them less energy to apply to their search for insight, self-awareness, and self-understanding and to building an appreciation for socially approved values. Anxiety can be useful in group counseling if it is converted to positive motivation. However, unnecessary and counterproductive anxiety is a wasteful drain.

Confidentiality

Few things can provoke uncontrolled anxiety more than uncertainty over how revelations will be treated. Will revelations, whether deliberately or accidentally made, be used exploitatively or destructively? Group members, at least initially, have no basis for trusting each other or the counselor. The experience of most group members, unfortunately, is that being open is tantamount to being vulnerable, and being vulnerable usually invites exploitation and hurt. There is no way to make the group comfortable unless and until the issue of how confidences will be respected, treated, and used is addressed by the counselor and the group.

Sometimes a revelation may be used to hide, screen, or mask an emotionally provocative issue. This can be true even when the revelation is especially dramatic or incendiary. Counselors should be cautious of even an emotionally charged revelation because the individual may be hiding more meaningful and emotionally turbulent feelings, needs, episodes, and impulses. Counselors shouldn't be distracted by what seems to be a deeply revealing "confession" because there is likely to be as much hidden as revealed.

The credibility of the group counseling process may depend on how the issue of confidentiality is handled. It would be naive to assume that group counseling can be effective unless the counselor follows the ethical requirements for not betraying a confidence. Nothing can undermine a session faster than a situation in which the group, in fact or fancy, believes the counselor cannot be trusted with confidential information. The counselor must indicate by word and deed that confidences will be respected with certain predefined limitations. On one hand, counselors are responsible for carrying out their ethical obligations to keep a confidence. On the other hand, in a correctional setting, counselors are legally responsible for bringing evidence and other vital information to the attention of the appropriate authorities. How, then, do counselors discharge their responsibilities to both?

The last thing counselors want is to be thought of as untrustworthy. It is natural for counselors to want to be liked and accepted. If counselors are weak or confused, it is possible that these needs will be exploited by some group members who sense this and who will attempt to manipulate these needs by making the counselor a coconspirator. By possessing guilty knowledge, which the counselor hides or does not reveal, he or she may become a coconspirator and be in serious trouble.

Usually, if individuals divulge important or confidential information about themselves of their own volition, it is safe to assume that it was no accident. If counselors make it clear from the beginning that they will not do anything of a destructive nature to any of the group members, and if their credibility is trusted by the group, they are in a good position to resolve the issue of confidentiality. It would be appropriate for the group counselor, in a private interview with the group member in question, to determine what the motives were that prompted the group member's disclosure. Because the group member had been informed from the beginning that the counselor could not withhold information vital to the authorities or vital to helping the group member, there is reason to suspect that the group member really wants such action to be taken despite protests to the contrary. In some cases, the reasons why he or she "slipped" may be more important to the counseling of the individual than the information divulged.

Although, in most cases, with tactful individual counseling, the group member may be induced to cooperate with the counselor to share the revealed information, it is possible that he or she may refuse. At this point, the counselor must make a choice. If the information is truly important, the counselor may have to reveal it. If this is the case, the counselor must be open and tell the individual that this action will be taken. In the long run, such candor is often respected. When it isn't, the counselor should be mature enough to understand what must be done and to face the consequences of carrying out his or her responsibilities, even when it is unpleasant to do so. Any less would be picked up by the group. On the surface, they may act as though the counselor is "one of the guys," but in truth, they know that he or she was not strong enough to do what should have been done. Group members may like the counselor, but they will not trust the counselor in any situation where it would be important for him or her to stand firm.

Confronting the issue of confidentiality can go a long way in relieving group tension. Two other ways to relieve tension are encouraging informality of expression and placing a premium on the degree of participation.

Encouraging participation places a premium on the value of each member's experiences, feelings, and needs. It also places a premium on pooling and sharing these with other members. When group members believe that what they have to say is important, that they are important as individuals, that others share their feelings, needs, and impulses, they tend to lose much of their hesitancy and defensive suspicion. For many participants, this is beyond anything they had ever thought possible. The counselor is responsible for building this atmosphere. To a great extent, how well the counselor does this will determine the success of his or her efforts at counseling.

Introducing the Session

The next step is for the counselor to introduce the session. The introduction should be brief, informal, factual, and informative. It establishes an atmosphere of open acceptance and close confidence.

The counselor's introduction of the session should include the following points:

- purpose of group counseling, what it is, why it is used

- what group counseling can and cannot do (this is especially important so that members do not expect any special cure, deal, pay-off, or reward that is not likely to grow out of participating in counseling)

- affirmation that each group member's contributions are welcomed and voluntary

- a warning that disputes may be tolerated only if they are verbal; they may not be acted out in a physically assaultive fashion either against person or property

- affirmation that members are not *required* to say anything but are encouraged to participate

- a warning that the counselor, unlike some members of clergy, has no legal protection for withholding any information that is evidentiary, even if it was revealed in confidence

- assurance that if the session is to be taped, the tape will be played back to the group before the session ends and any member may have any of his or her statements or evidence of his or her presence erased from the tape should he or she so choose

- any benefits members derive from group counseling depend on how much they are willing and able to help themselves and to accept help from others

- although the counselor may present some suggestions as to what the group might discuss, the group is encouraged to decide discussion topics for themselves

- announcement of the exact time the session will end (and stick to this time no matter what)

- assurance that if the group is ready for additional sessions, these sessions will be scheduled

- any member who wishes a private interview with the counselor can have this arranged promptly

- affirmation that members may use language with which they feel comfortable (Many individuals in counseling have a marked deficiency in verbal skills. Frequently they have thoughts, feelings, and needs for which they have difficulty finding words. It is not unusual to find that a major result of this is the use of slang and profanity or, when rage goes beyond verbal skill, an explosion of violence expressing the rage that words could not express. If the counselor insists that group members use "acceptable English," they may feel inhibited. Valuable expressions may be kept back, squelched, modified, or lost completely.)

- assurance that any group member may raise any questions; there are no taboo topics

In terms of topics, there may be a greater problem with administrative, managerial, and line staff sensitivity than with the sensitivity of group members. For example, it is not unusual for staff who are not involved in group counseling to be concerned about "what's being said in that room." There are occasional "blockbusters" that group members reveal about a staff member. Often, if there is any substance to this disclosure, it is magnified and distorted. However, it should not be disregarded by the counselor or his or her supervisor; the disclosure should be investigated.

If malfeasance is alleged, it must be checked out, however dangerous or unpleasant it may be to do so. To avoid having group counseling sessions turn into forums for voicing allegations of malfeasance, counselors should indicate to group members, from the start, that the major function of group counseling is not to provide opportunities to "snitch" on staff members but to provide a series of opportunities for group members to develop self-awareness, self-understanding, and skills at using socially acceptable and productive behavioral alternatives. If a legitimate avenue for voicing grievances is otherwise available, it should be used instead of group counseling for such purposes. If such an avenue has not been established, it should be so that programs are not diverted from their intended purposes.

The delivery of these opening introductory statements is one of the few times the counselor will be doing most of the talking. Beyond this, it is up to the counselor to reinforce these ground rules by the manner in which he or she conducts the session. Counselors should not fall into speech making in the opening, closing, or during the session. The session is no place for long-winded, sermonizing oration on the part of the counselor.

Many new counselors are tempted to talk too much during sessions. This is natural and understandable and is usually motivated by a desire to convey some idea or value to the group. It is especially the case when new counselors don't have much faith in the ability of the group to develop these discussions and concepts for itself, even with their indirect help. Counselors should give group members time and have faith in their capabilities; they'll usually come through when they are ready. If not now, then later.

It isn't necessary to give the group all of the answers. Counselors should not be talking when they should be listening, and listening creatively. Counselors are, after all, enablers. What they say or do, or refrain from saying or doing, should be directed toward helping the group function, learn, develop, and grow.

Words and deeds are some of the tools of the counselor. The effectiveness of any tool is compromised if it is used beyond the point where it has any relevance to the job it was meant to do. The secret of success in counseling can be likened to the secret of taking a cold shower: quick in and quick out. The purpose of the session is to address the needs of the members, not those of the counselor.

The Importance of Flexibility

Most beginners tend to feel more secure and comfortable when they have hard and fast rules and regulations to guide them. They become somewhat suspicious of a situation in which flexibility is a requirement. For example, when driving through a new and unfamiliar area, most drivers tend to feel more at ease if the area is clearly marked by street names and route numbers. They are even more secure if they have a road map with explicit directions that are easily followed. They are certainly more at ease than those who must drive through an unmarked and unfamiliar area without even a rudimentary road map.

It is natural to try to cling to the familiar, to develop formulas, rules, and regulations that act as guides. With specific guideposts, it is not as easy to get lost or make mistakes than if there were no guides at all. Beginners, in particular, take great comfort from the concrete and become worried with the abstract and the flexible. This is the way many beginners in group counseling feel. It is important to remember that most beginners go through the same emotions.

In group counseling, a premium is placed on flexibility as opposed to formula. Many beginners are tempted to formularize their methods and techniques because doing so makes them feel more comfortable when leading a group counseling session. A boxer with a routine approach seldom gets beyond being a "prelim" fighter. The beginner in group counseling, to get beyond the preliminaries, has to resist the urge to operate by a hard and fast formula. He or she has to be flexible in method and approach. For many beginners, the struggle against the desire to develop a formularized approach is difficult, but it can be done.

There are specific reasons why flexibility is so important to group counseling. Human beings and the situations in which they find themselves are fluid and flexible. Because people and situations are in constantly changing interrelationships, the group counselor's technique must reflect a great deal of flexibility. In group situations, especially, these changes may occur dramatically or discreetly, not only from session to session but also from moment to moment in the same session.

Group and individual needs, goals, interests, motivations, and responses may be affected by such changes. It is important for group counselors to appreciate these changes and deal with them. A rigid and unyielding approach will not adjust to these changes.

Efficient group counselors are flexible, with certain qualifications. Even a good thing can be overdone. This is especially true if the counselor confuses flexibility with total permissiveness that does not define directions, goals, and areas the group might explore productively.

In a short-term group counseling program, sessions must be all meat and no potatoes. This means that little time can be devoted to going off on tangents in the session. The counselor should avoid the extremes of restricting content so much that the session becomes rigid or of being so flexible that the session drifts and becomes unproductive.

The counselor is responsible for maintaining the thread of the session to help the group have a productive experience. The counselor also helps the group develop meaningful program content, with the accent on "help." The counselor doesn't do the job for the group, but enables the group to do the job for itself.

To aid this process, the group counselor does the following:

- encourages each member to participate

- helps members learn how to express themselves, but doesn't do it for them

- gives full recognition to individuals for each positive contribution made to the process, no matter how slight

- points out areas related to the discussion the group might profitably explore

- accepts the individual for what he or she is, but doesn't necessarily approve of what the person has done

- shares with the group his or her own experiences that relate to the subject of discussion

- by his or her attitude, teaches group members to accept each other and to value each other's positive contributions

- makes himself or herself, as a personality, accessible to the group and to each group member

- provides a firm, stable, and security-giving foundation,

especially for those who have never before experienced this

Turning Questions into Discussion

After introducing the session, the counselor may invite questions from the group. There is no pattern to the questions the counselor may expect from group members. Questions may relate to what was presented by the counselor or they may be without apparent relevance. It is important for the counselor to inquire into and determine the meanings of issues or questions raised by the group or one of its members. Unless the counselor has insight into what is really being implied or transmitted by a question or other response (a non-response is also a response, paradoxically), he or she may well go off on a tangent that will convince the group of his or her lack of sensitivity.

For example, suppose a group member asked the counselor—out of nowhere—"Mr. Jones, did you ever steal?" Why would the member ask such a question? What was he or she really looking for? The following are some possibilities:

1. The individual wished to gain status with the group.

2. The individual wished to receive attention.

3. He or she was feeling angry with and suspicious of people in authority and this was his or her way of trying to express this to the counselor who, at that moment, represented authority.

4. He or she was suspicious that the counselor was "fronting" by creating a false image of being without blemish and, therefore, "better" than the group members.

5. He or she was interested in whether or not straight people are always straight or just part-time straight.

6. He or she was interested in whether or not the counselor had ever faced the temptations and impulses that he or she had. Have other people failed? Is he or she different? Is the counselor different?

7. He or she wanted to know if the counselor's feet are made of clay, if the counselor is human after all.

8. He or she was uncomfortable in his or her anticipation of the session and was seeking to divert the counselor with a

provocative question. If this were successful, pressure would be taken from the group member because while the counselor is talking, and the group member doesn't have to.

How to handle the question depends on what's behind it, so the first step is to find out. One way is to be direct and ask. The counselor may say, "I'll answer your question in just a moment if you wish, but your question interests me. Can you tell me why you asked it?" This response turns the situation around. It's now the group member's turn. The questioner might reply, "I just don't think there are any honest people...I mean people who've never lied and never stole." The counselor could then turn to the other group members and ask them what they think of this statement. A lively discussion can be triggered in which the group could bring up the following points:

1. Almost everyone lies or steals at one time or another.

2. "The difference between us and 'honest' people is that we kept on doing it, many times and often. 'Honest' people, if they did something wrong, did only small things, like steal a candy bar or run a red light. Or if they did something real bad, didn't do it so they'd get caught."

3. "Power makes the difference. Those who don't have power get messed up if they break the law. Even if those who have power get caught, they don't get punished like those of us who don't have power. Being poor means having no power."

4. "Either you're lucky or you ain't. If your luck is running good and you get your act together, you can break the law and get away with it, and your reputation might be just as good as if you were a goody-goody."

The group might grapple with this question for the whole session. At the end of the session, the counselor should summarize what the group has said, being fair to all points of view that have been expressed. Because the issue of what is or is not criminal or delinquent is very complex, the group may wish to pick up on this point at the next session. How honest must a person be to be considered honest? Is it a case of all or nothing? The session should end at the time stated at the beginning, with the counselor thanking group members for their contributions to the session.

In this case, by reversing the role of respondent from himself or herself back to the group member, the counselor provoked a full-scale discussion. By involving the group, the counselor enlarged the scope of participation. The group member's initial question and responses revealed a great deal about himself or herself and his or her thinking. Each group member was able to gain insight on how other group members felt about this issue.

Discussion provided a chance for each person to test the genuineness of what every other person claimed as his or her position. One session is unlikely to "rehabilitate" anyone, but a process was stimulated and initiated that, if ultimately successful, might benefit not only the questioner but others in the group.

Introducing Discussion Topics

Time is a more important factor in short-term group counseling than in the traditional and extended group counseling format. The short-term format requires the counselor to be more assertive and more directive because there is less time to wait out the group. The counselor who conducts short-term group counseling actively primes the group to provide stimulating and provocative elements that can provoke reaction and response. The use of discussion topics is one way to do this.

When, during the initial stage of the session, the counselor is at the point where discussion topics are to be introduced to the group, he or she must exercise some degree of sensitivity. Group members will be watching for clues that indicate what the counselor would like them to say or how he or she would like them to react. Everyone has a set of biases, preferences, attitudes, needs, and values. The group will be quick to spot these if the counselor doesn't carefully select and phrase the topics proposed for discussion.

There are no right or wrong responses that the counselor should expect from the group—even if these responses are the same as those the counselor would make. Counselors must understand that all the responses the group may make are legitimate and significant. Counselors should not assume that if the group mirrors their beliefs, the group has made the right response.

Group members should be encouraged to respond in ways that are meaningful to them—not merely as an echo of the counselor's beliefs. Therefore, discussion topics should not be selected, presented, or phrased in such a way as to lead or skew the group members' responses so that they do not reflect the group so much as the group's conformation to clues consciously or unconsciously expressed by the counselor.

The case of a new counselor who presents, as a suggestion for discussion, the topic "Success or Failure" can illustrate this point. Suppose this counselor has a very strong need to be successful. Did the counselor present the topic of "Success or Failure" as a reflection of his or her own needs or as a result of an analysis of the needs and readiness of the group?

Even if the selection of this topic was valid, the counselor in this illustration might easily betray his or her own concerns about success and failure by phrasing the topic's issues in such a way as to indicate these concerns to the group. For example, the counselor might indicate this by saying, "How can we keep from failing? How can we be successful?" This phrasing can indicate his or her biases and needs.

A neutral way of phrasing encourages the group to explore meanings and values for themselves and, once explored, to express them and to examine the consequences that can flow from each option. A neutral way of phrasing this topic might be: "Success and failure: What do they mean to you?" Yet another way to involve the group would be through the counselor's recalling of some recent events in which group members participated. In the process, the counselor may ask group members to analyze the events and the responses, asking them to evaluate what they think was a successful or unsuccessful response and why. This could then lead to a discussion of the implications that grow out of success and failure, which, in turn, could lead to deeper explorations.

The emphasis in group counseling is placed on exploratory contributions, sharing and risking self-revelation, achieving understanding, and learning how to apply these understandings to one's daily life. It is not placed on the ability to tell the counselor what he or she may want to hear. Even if the counselor could do so, it would not be appropriate to remake the group in his or her own image. The goal is to help each member become a more effective and wholesome person and not a carbon copy of the counselor. After having introduced three or four topics (as options for discussion rather than as mandates), the counselor should also state affirmatively that any group member may propose another option. The group is not limited to the options proposed by the counselor.

Group members may avail themselves of the freedom to propose other options, or they may not. It is their choice, and how they exercise

Even if a counselor could do so, it would not be appropriate to remake the group in his or her own image.

this choice may, in itself, be of significance to the understanding of the group dynamic if the counselor can find out why they made the choice.

For example, suppose a counselor was conducting a group session in a facility for juvenile offenders being held for court adjudication. After the counselor presented a few discussion options, a group member spoke up and presented an additional option: the fear of facing the judge, of appearing in court. The counselor's first response was to ask why this topic was of interest. One member replied that the day before, twelve juveniles had gone to court and, of these, nine had been sentenced to correctional institutions. Another member then blurted out, "And we go to court tomorrow. What chance do we have?" This precipitated a very valuable and productive counseling session in an area not proposed or even sensed by the counselor.

This example illustrates how important it is for counselors to be aware of current concerns, issues, and events involving the group. Using these as precipitants, motivators, and propellants of counseling response has a proven effectiveness in most, but not all, instances. It is less effective in circumstances where fear or anxiety require members to deny, hide, or mask interest, knowledge, or concern.

Counselors must feel sufficiently relaxed with what they are doing so that they can wait a reasonable amount of time for the group to formulate its choices and opinions. Members don't have to be speaking all the time. Counselors should not feel compelled to fill in all the gaps in the conversation. They should encourage participation from group members, but they shouldn't participate for them. If gaps do occur, give group members time. They may need time to digest some of the meanings and implications of what has transpired, or they may need time to gather courage to face the next phase.

If the Group Is Resistant

Sometimes, despite the counselor's attempts to motivate and encourage the group, the group just doesn't seem to want to do much talking. The counselor may call the group's attention to this and state that if the group doesn't feel like having a session at that time, perhaps they might feel better about it the next time a session is scheduled.

If, in the judgment of the counselor, the session is not productive or likely to become so, he or she may end it. If this action is taken, the counselor should explain it to the group. After all, it is quite reasonable to expect that, at certain times, people may not feel like talking or relating.

The counselor may recognize this, but it is important to find out why the group does not feel like talking, because this, too, is a response. There can be any number of reasons and explanations—usually there are several rather than just one—and each is important to understanding what is happening with and to the group and its members.

For example, suppose one of the group members had been homosexually assaulted. Although it may have happened a couple of days prior to the counseling session and all of the group members are aware of the details, as is the counselor, the group may be edgy and unable to confront this event and the issues surrounding it until some time later, after the victim has been able to relate and level some of his or her feelings in the privacy of case counseling sessions.

If counselors must terminate the session under these circumstances, they should let the group know that they understand and can accept the situation. Counselors should neither feel nor act as though they or their skills have been attacked, impugned, or insulted. It is possible that new counselors may feel very anxious or threatened when this occurs. With time, counselors learn that the group acts a particular way because of the group dynamics that are operating at the time. Perhaps the next try will be different because the group dynamics will be different.

Ways of Opening Discussion

There are many ways, methods, and devices that can be used to motivate, encourage, and develop discussions in group counseling. Any method or gimmick is only as good as the counselor who employs it. Good results have been obtained with a number of methods, but

Chalkboards or flipcharts are effective tools.

good counselors can frequently obtain good results irrespective of the methods they may use.

Counselors are only fooling themselves if they rely on gimmicks rather than their own sensitivity, awareness, and disciplined concern. Gimmicks are not magical charms that accomplish good results when counselors are inadequate in the role of counselor. Even the best tools are effective only in the hands of a craftsman. Methods and devices are some of the tools of the counselor. They can help a good counselor be better, but they are not what makes the counselor.

Chalkboards or flipcharts are effective tools. Counselors may use a chalkboard to write down topics, pertinent and important points, and illustrative material. For example, when a group member makes a significant contribution, the counselor may wish to write it on the chalkboard. This rewards the contributor, emphasizes the point, focuses group attention on it, and may even encourage others to add to it or contribute new points. The chalkboard serves as a positive reinforcer. By inference, points that the counselor does not write down may be attenuated, inhibited, or reduced by not being written by the counselor. How the counselor uses this device may enhance his or her role of orchestrating the session. Whether or not the counselor writes down a point made by a member may, of itself, become a counseling issue of significance.

Slides, movies, and other audiovisual aids may be used. These can provoke discussion or be particularly illustrative of a special point the counselor may wish the group to explore. Audiovisual materials should be properly screened for appropriateness and potential, then cleared with the supervisor before the session.

In evaluating audiovisual materials, some of the following issues might be considered:

1. Is the point or message straightforward and clear?

2. Is it attention-getting in the way it communicates the message?

3. Is the information it imparts correct and factual?

4. Is the information imparted on a level with the target group? Over their heads? Under their level and, perhaps, patronizing? Just right?

5. Is there a main message, and does it stand out from other messages and issues?

6. Are the issues presented in a way that is easily understood and not confusing?

7. If there is music or another language being communicated, is it at the level of the target group?

8. Is there room for the beliefs, values, and convictions of the target group or is the message absolute?

9. Is there a step-by-step presentation of the issues, problems, alternatives, and the probable consequences for each alternative?

10. Is the material sympathetic to and understanding of the cultural variables on which differing values are based?

11. Does the material present itself in a way in which the target group can feel that there is concern for them?

12. Is this the best way to present the issues, or should this be used to reinforce issues developed and presented in another way?

13. Is the material overly elegant or simplistic in its implication that change is easy to accomplish?

14. Does the material promise more than is realistic, given the setting?

An audio or video cassette or record player may also be used. For example, an audio cassette may be played, either instrumental or vocal, and the group may be asked to give its impressions or express the feelings engendered by listening to the cassette. Photographs may be used to provoke expression of feelings, needs, beliefs, and values. Written material may also be used effectively. A newspaper article, a short story, a letter, a memo, a bulletin board notice, biographies, or autobiographies all can be used to stimulate group reaction, response, and participation or illustrate points that are important to counseling. Libraries are full of such material, geared to all age groups. The use of such devices can be quite stimulating. The group's use of these materials can frequently be productive.

The use of hypothetical situations may also provide stimulation for the group. These situations can be presented to the group either in written form or by the counselor in story-telling fashion. The following are some sample situations:

1. There was a teenage girl whose parents argued and fought with each other often. Things kept getting worse. The teenager told no one how she felt.

   a. Why?
   b. How do you suppose she felt?
   c. What could she do about the situation?
   d. What would you do in her place?

2. A teacher noticed a student sitting toward the back of the room. The child was crying. "Why are you crying?" asked the teacher. The child said, "Some kids on the playground hit me." The teach said that this was silly and told the child to stop crying. The child did. The child did not tell the teacher that the real reason for the crying was that the child's father left home, maybe never to return.

   a. How do you feel about this?
   b. If you were the child, what would you do?
   c. If you were the teacher, what would you do?
   d. What advice would you give the child? Why?

3. A young man had never known his father, not even his father's name. One day, he overheard a relative mention this information.

   a. What should he do?
   b. If you were in his place, what would you do?
   c. Was it right for relatives to keep this hidden from him?

4. A young man had never known his father. One day, a man appeared at the door and said, "I am your father."

   a. If you were in this young man's place, what would you do? Why?
   b. If you were in the father's place, what would you do? Why?

5. A man had gotten into trouble with the law. Others involved in the offense were given probation, but he was committed to an institution. "Did the judge especially dislike me?" he wondered. "Does my group like me because I did their time for them? When I get out, what will the neighborhood think of me?"

   a. If you were this person, what would you do?

b. How would you feel?

6. A girl painted a picture in school and brought it home to show the family—especially Mom. When she got home, the first thing she did was to go up to Mom and say to her, "Look what I did in school." Mom replied, "Don't bother me!"

   a. If you were this girl, how would you feel?
   b. What would you do?
   c. What would you say?

7. One day while out walking with his family, a boy tripped and fell, slightly scraping a knee. Tears came to his eyes, especially when Dad said, "Stop crying, you big dope!"

   a. If you were this boy, what would you do?
   b. What would you say?

8. A boy seemed to have a lot of trouble keeping up with the rest of the class in schoolwork. It seemed as though almost all of the students learned things faster and knew more. One day, while reciting in class, he made a mistake. Everyone started laughing.

   a. If you were this boy, how would you feel?
   b. What would you do?

9. A young man had an important problem. He went home and told Mom about it in confidence. Mom seemed to take it very seriously. A few days later, he overheard Mom telling the story to a neighbor, and both of them were having a good laugh.

   a. If you were this young man, how would you feel?
   b. If the situation were reversed, and it was your parents who heard you making light of their problems, what would you do?

10. A young woman had parents who were separated. The young woman lived with Mom, but didn't get along with her at all. She went to live with Dad, who was a hero in her eyes. One day, while she and her dad were shopping in a department store, she saw her dad shoplifting. The father did not realize his daughter saw him do this.

    a. If you were this young woman, how would you feel?

b. Suppose the situations were reversed, and your father spotted you shoplifting. What would you do? What would you say?

11. A young man out walking with a group of friends spotted his mother staggering out of a bar. All his friends knew she was his mother.

    a. If you were this young man, how would you feel?
    b. What would you say?
    c. How would you feel if the situation were reversed?

12. A young woman had no home of her own. She lived with the family of one of her friends. They were kind to her and, most of the time, everything went well. Then she became careless. She showered only when she was told. Her table manners became worse. She was damaging or breaking small things around the house and dropping papers or trash. In her bedroom she had chipped paint and plaster from some spots on the walls. She scratched her initials on one of the chairs in the living room. The family wondered what to do about it. They did not like to be around her because she did not shower regularly, and she had body odor. They could not allow their house to be damaged and their personal property broken.

    a. What could they do about it?
    b. If they told her, would it hurt her feelings?
    c. Should they allow her to continue?
    d. If the family decided to tell her, how should they go about it?

13. A teenage girl had a friend who had a bad reputation in the neighborhood. This girl's parents wanted to break up the friendship.

    a. Why?
    b. What would you do if you were the girl?
    c. What would you tell your friend?
    d. What would you do if you were this girl's friend?

14. A young man had a group of friends who decided to hold a party. This young man's parents said, "You can't go because the last time you went out with them you got into trouble."

    a. What would you have done or said if you were the parents?

    b. What would you have done or said if you were this young man?

    c. How would you have felt?

    d. What would you tell your friends?

15. A woman had several friends who always seemed to have spending money. This woman hardly ever had as much spending money as her friends. One day, the group decided to go out to a movie and then maybe go out for a pizza. The problem was that this would cost more money than the woman had.

    a. What would you do if you were this woman?

    b. How would you feel?

16. A student got a part in a school play. The play was to be put on at a school assembly, and all of the parents were invited. Almost all the parents came except this student's. When the play was over, one of the parents of a classmate came up to this student and said, "You did very well, it's too bad your folks weren't here to see you. I wouldn't have missed seeing you for the world!"

    a. If you were this student, what would you do?

    b. How would you feel?

17. A boy had several brothers and sisters. Every time something went wrong, it seemed that the only one who got blamed was this boy, as though the brothers and sisters were always angels. One day, one of the brothers got into trouble.

    a. If you were the boy and it was your brother, "the angel," who had gotten in trouble, what would you say?

    b. How would you feel?

18. One day a student got into a fight with a classmate. Although the student had started the fight, it was the classmate who finished it. Everybody saw that this student came out second best. When this student got home, Mom said, "How did you tear your shirt?"

    a. If you were this student, how would you feel?

    b. What would you say?

c. What would you do?

19. A young man came from a very poor family. He was invited to a formal dance, but he didn't have nice enough clothes to attend. A neighbor said, "My son grew out of these clothes, and they're hardly worn. Why don't you take them and wear them?" The young man took them, but later found out that the neighbor had told practically everybody about the clothes.

   a. If you were this young man, what would you do?
   b. How would you feel?
   c. What would you say?

20. A girl came from a poor family. Her shoes had holes in them. Mom said, "Visit your aunt, and ask her for shoes. She has money and can buy them for you." The girl went to see her aunt, who had company. The aunt said, "Hold up your foot, and let me see your shoe." When the niece did this, the aunt said, for the guests to hear, "Look how this child's mother lets this kid go around," and all the guests were invited to take a look at the holes in this girl's shoes.

   a. If you were this girl, what would you do?
   b. How would you feel?
   c. What would you say?

21. A girl lived in a neighborhood that had a very bad reputation. Her parents worked hard to save enough money so that the family could move to a better neighborhood. The girl was happy in this new neighborhood, and she made many friends. She never told her new friends where she had lived before. In every way, she acted and talked like her new friends, and they never suspected. Then another new girl moved into the neighborhood, but everybody knew that this girl had moved from a bad neighborhood. They were saying unkind things about her and where she had come from.

   a. What should the first girl do?
   b. How do you suppose she felt?
   c. What would you have done if you were in her place?

22. A young man found out that his parents were worried and upset about an important problem. He went to his father

and asked, "Is there any way I can help?" The father replied, "It's none of your business."

a. If you were this young man, how would you feel?
b. What would you do or say?

23. A boy had an older brother who seemed to be the best in everything he did. Wherever the boy went, no matter what he did, people would be sure to say that they had seen his older brother do it better. Even his parents said this.

a. If you were this boy, how would you feel?
b. What would you do?

24. A young man had been getting into trouble with the law. The time came when the court had no choice but to send him to an institution. Week after week while he was at the institution, he saw other detainees receiving many visits from their families. No one ever came to visit him. He was worried.

a. Why was he worried?
b. If you were this young man, how would you feel?
c. What would you do?

The use of hypothetical stories compiled by the counselor can be augmented by stories supplied by group members with encouragement from the counselor. In this way, the material more closely relates to the actual concerns and experiences of the group. Motivational material can be produced by creative effort. The only limits on its production are those imposed by the creative ingenuity of the counselor.

Keeping the Session Moving

Counselors are responsible for keeping the session moving. They may do this by the following:

- guarding against unrelated tangents

- encouraging all members of the group to participate

- giving credit to individuals for all contributions, however small

- taking time out at appropriate points in the session to

A well-conducted staff development program can help the staff person understand that the roles of counselor and correctional officer do not conflict.

summarize what had been said up to that point, being fair to each point of view

- pointing out related areas or issues that the group might explore

- encouraging the expression of different points of view

- tactfully discouraging "soap box" oration, including their own

- patiently helping members express themselves if they are floundering in the attempt

Some Typical Group Reactions

How a group reacts may mean little to counselors unless they are able to understand and appreciate the situation in which the reaction occurred.

At times, the context of the situation provides clues as to the meaning of events that have taken place. For example, many of us have probably had the experience of dealing with a particular shopkeeper for years. One day, while walking down the street we may see a vaguely familiar person. It is the same shopkeeper with whom we've dealt for so long, but we're used to seeing him only in one context: in his shop. Outside of that context, he is recognizable only with some effort.

By the same token, in the counseling context, counselors are relating to the group somewhat differently than when they are outside of the counseling session. This is especially true when group counselors are recruited from the ranks of careworkers, correctional officers, instructors, and other occupations whose usual duties had not previously included counseling. In such cases, these staff conduct group counseling in addition to their usual duties, not in place of them.

Counselors recruited from the security force, for example, may behave differently as correctional officers than they would as counselors. This difference in behavior may confuse group members. It may also confuse the staff person, especially if the relationships between these roles are not clearly appreciated or if they are seen as conflicting.

A well-conducted staff development program can help the staff person understand that although the roles of correctional officer and counselor are different, they do not conflict with each other. In fact, everyone wears many hats and engages in different roles. A man may be husband, father, breadwinner, disciplinarian, friend, etc., and may act somewhat differently in each role, but basically he is the same person and, through him, these roles are related to each other.

In a prison setting, for example, inmates may benefit from seeing correctional officers in counseling roles. It may dispel some stereotypes, and the inmates may get an entirely new and expanded understanding of this staff person. It may also benefit correctional officers to see inmates not only as custody and security problems, but also as people with very human needs, feelings, struggles, and hopes—a view more readily seen in a counseling context than on the cellblock.

Attitudes and feelings may change when individuals have a newer and more complete picture of the people with whom they have been interacting. When inmates see correctional officers only as correctional officers, they have a flat and one-dimensional understanding of them as human beings. When inmates see correctional officers function in additional roles, they take on additional human dimensions. This is also true of correctional officers' view of inmates. In this learning process, there is the potential for growth for both group members and counselors. For these reasons alone, group counseling can be a valid and valuable program element, independent of the effectiveness of treatment programs in general.

However, people enter the group counseling experience with all of their experiences and biases. Group reactions in counseling depend on many things: the newness of the situation, the composition of the group, and past group and individual experiences. Whether or not the session was held before or after mealtime, before or after recreation, before or after a movie, or any number of similar situations will affect the group's reactions in counseling. Did any of the members receive disciplinary action prior to the session? Did someone in the session fail to get a letter or an expected visit?

The answers to these and similar questions will bear directly on how the group may react in counseling. The following are some typical group reactions encountered by counselors:

1. Signs of anxiety, such as giggling, shifting of feet and posture, sweating, watchful and intense waiting, clearing of throats, heavy breathing, silence or unusual noisiness, fidgeting, etc., may be shown.

2. Some members may seem unusually bright and alert; some may seem dull and lethargic. Sometimes the group seems indifferent, while at other times, it seems intensely interested.

3. The group may seek to take the initiative and present several questions to the counselor.

4. Group members may behave in an overly assertive and aggressive fashion, griping about everything under the sun, including the counselor, attacking him or her either directly or indirectly. They may say, "You're going to counsel us? What did you ever do to become a counselor?" implying that the counselor is unqualified. A statement like this one is calculated to get a rise out of the counselor. They may say, "You're acting like a psychiatrist.... Psychiatrists think everybody is crazy, asking all those fruity questions." Here the group states its low opinion of a profession, then tries to equate the counselor with that profession. Or the group

may try to turn the table on the counselor by saying, "What do you mean by honesty? Don't tell us that you ain't never stole nothing!"

5. Sometimes things *do* go well, and a good session seems to flow from the outset.

Group members, through some of these devices, may be testing the counselor, the counseling situation, each other, or all of these things. Or group members may be venting—that is, getting some excess anxiety off their chests. The excess anxiety may have been produced well before the session rather than because of it. Resistance by group members may be better handled by understanding the dynamics of the group.

A group's dynamics usually are very complex and not easily analyzed. Each person's reaction is affected by a number of the internal and external stimuli taking place before and during the session—only some of which may be known by the counselor. This is why it may be helpful for counselors and their supervisors to review the session. Information gathered from these reviews may then be used to plan future sessions.

In any event, if properly handled, group reactions can be used constructively. The trick is not to rise to the bait but determine why the bait was cast. This may not be perceived by the counselor during the session but may become clear when the session is reviewed.

The introduction of a new topic or any new element may heighten any of the aforementioned reactions. Many of these reactions are highly defensive and wasteful. When group members learn that they do not need to invest so much energy in defense, they are then able to apply their energies to developing insights and achieving positive potential.

VI. Special Methods and Techniques

The arsenal of professional tools, that is, the methods and techniques of counseling used in short-term group counseling, is fairly large. In selecting or developing methods and techniques, counselors should keep in mind that, irrespective of methods or technique, good counselors will get good results. Methods and techniques are tools—and tools are only as productive as those who use them. Professional tools may be of great help to counselors, but they won't do the job for them.

Why are so many methods and techniques needed? This is like asking carpenters why they need a variety of tools. Each tool is calculated to do a special job. Sometimes tools are interchangeable in that they may serve a similar function. In such a case, the preferences of the craftsmen and the comparative efficiency of the tools determine the choice. This is no less true of the professional tools of the group counselor.

Methods and techniques of group counseling are manifold. This is a happy circumstance in that choices available to group counselors are limitless. Once having made their choice, however, counselors are not limited by that choice. They are still free to change methods and techniques. There may be any number of reasons for doing this. At times, doing so may be a requirement inherent in the group situation. Some reasons for change may include the following:

- a change in situation

- a change in group interests, needs, goals, attitudes, motivation, or any combination of these

- introduction of new and different material or subject matter

- a change in group composition, relationships, or level of understanding and maturity

- a change in group anxiety level

- a change in the counselor's feelings, needs, motives, attitudes, goals, or relationships with the group or self

- a change in the group's feelings toward the counselor

Even if no appreciable changes take place, counselors may wish to encourage more movement through a change in method and/or technique. Counselors may wish to try something new and different just to see what will happen—test a new approach.

There are many other reasons that may encourage or necessitate the use of additional or substitute methods and techniques. At times, this has to be accomplished on the spot, in the session, with no opportunity for the counselor to plan. This is one of the challenges of group counseling.

If, however, counselors have sufficient forewarning and have an opportunity to plan such changes, they should discuss it with their supervisor, who can help and advise. With all counselors going through this process, it is important that each counselor share his or her experience, not only with his or her supervisor but with fellow counselors as well. Each may then be able to profit from the other's efforts, failures, and successes. This is what is meant by team effort.

With each change of method and technique, there will be some changes in the counselor, the group, and the counseling situation. These changes may run the gamut from dramatic to insignificant, but there will be changes. Although a major change in what the counselor is doing may result in a major change in the session, this does not always happen. At times, a minute change can cause a big reverberation and vice-versa. Group counseling sessions as a result of this process are seldom static and placid. Everything is usually in motion at the same time. This is another challenge of group counseling.

Role-taking and Role-reversal

Role-taking and role-reversal are two valuable techniques used to help group members get a better understanding of how other people might feel in certain situations. These techniques, when successfully used, provide group members with the chance to psychologically walk in someone else's shoes.

Many people who have difficulty in their relationships with others and with society have some deficiencies in their capacities to feel along with others. If this deficiency is great enough, they become more isolated from other people; they do not feel "related" to others.

People become this way for several reasons. For example, in a situation where a group of black children was observed at play, one child said to the others, "Let's play explorer." Another child agreed and said, "And we're going to go where no other white man has gone before!" It was clear that these children had been so conditioned, they could not imagine that one could be both an explorer and black. They had to first imagine themselves as white before they could imagine themselves as explorers.

The effects of racism had begun to limit the imagination and aspiration of these children. Children learn by taking on imaginary roles and playing at them. Racism narrowed this process for these children and, by this, narrowed their potential for "feeling along" with a role of another person. When this happens not just to one role but to a great many, individuals may develop an incomplete understanding of these roles and a comparably diminished sense of identification with people who fill them. This is one of the ways people can become more iso-

Hurt after hurt can drive people into themselves.

lated from those around them. When this happens, they understand less and less about how they feel, and they care less and less.

Exposure to brutality and deprivation can, over the long run, also produce this sense of unrelatedness to people. Hurt after hurt can drive people into themselves and emotionally isolate and insulate them from others. There are also varieties of social and psychological pathology that can produce this. Whenever this happens, it produces individuals who may lack appreciation for what they have done to others and the seriousness of their conduct. When others object or react strongly to this conduct, these individuals are often amazed and genuinely do not understand why people are reacting to them in such a way. This is one of many reasons why some offenders do not appreciate the feelings of their victims.

For some of these people, role-taking and role-reversal in group counseling provide insights and, if these insights are used properly, amelioration.

Role-taking is when the counselor encourages group members to act out key roles in a hypothetical, but emotionally provocative, situation. Once the situation is acted out, those who observed the performance are asked to comment about what they observed or felt about how the role-takers handled themselves as compared with the role-takers' versions of how they felt at the time. The session is similar to an unrehearsed dramatic presentation. The counselor may substitute members for each role in the drama until every group member has had a chance to role-take as well as observe. Some members may even have a chance at more than one role.

Role-reversal is a more dimensional variety of role-taking. It is like turning a sock inside out. If, in role-taking, one member had been playing the role of a parent, for example, he or she might then switch roles with the member who had been playing the role of the child. This allows each member to develop a dimensional understanding of the interaction between parent and child, how each felt, and how these feelings contributed to the shaping of interaction. This may be done with any number of complementary roles, such as victim-aggressor, teacher-student, brother-sister, friend-friend, friend-enemy, boss-employee, husband-wife, boyfriend-girlfriend, etc.

The use of hand puppets in connection with role-taking and role-reversal might be productive because it offers individuals the defense that "It's not me saying this, it's the puppet." As a result, members may express themselves more freely. When a cassette recorder is used in connection with this device, the playback strips away the puppet, and only the voices are left. This usually results in a session loaded with meaningful material that contains enough meat for several exploratory sessions.

Taping the Session

Occasionally, the counselor may wish to tape the sessions. The use of a cassette recorder, under certain conditions, may stimulate and encourage group participation. Under other conditions, it may well have a limiting effect.

The limiting effect is not entirely without merit. Counseling is not the same as therapy. Basically, the difference is that although both share ego-supportive and reeducative functions, therapy, and not counseling, has a reconstructive function. Reconstruction is a process dealing with the basic building blocks of personality—identifying them, understanding them, seeing how they are arranged, seeing how the arrangement came to be, understanding how the arrangement affects behavior, and attempting to rearrange these building blocks to bring about behavioral change. Some of these building blocks are of an exceptionally intimate and private nature, hidden deep within the psyche of the individual. Handling this material requires exceptional skill and training. A cassette recorder may inhibit group members from making overly self-revealing statements that may be better handled in therapy. In this sense, a cassette recorder may prevent the content of the session from getting beyond the depth of skill of the counselor, who is not a therapist and should not attempt to be one. In addition to acting as a safety mechanism that inhibits (usually, but not always) deep self-revelation, a cassette recorder may act as a reinforcer of the reeducative process that may have taken place during the session. Everyone knows the story of the man who didn't appreciate what he had to say until he heard himself saying it. This happens with group members when the cassettes of their sessions are played back to them. During the playback, group members may anticipate statements about to be played and then point to whoever is about to be heard speaking next on the cassette. It is not uncommon for group members to gain insight on the rehearing that was not achieved when the statement was made during the session. In the process of rehearing, the group and its members are their own teachers.

Counselors should consider carefully how they might introduce the idea of recording to the group. Unless the cassette recorder is carefully introduced and employed, the group may feel, and with reason, that the confidential quality of the session is being compromised. The most successful way to introduce the cassette recorder to the group is to adopt the following techniques:

1. Well before the session, let the group know that a cassette recorder will be used.

2. Explain that the cassette recorder will be used to give group members a chance to hear what they sound like and what they've said.

3. Explain that the cassette can be erased in its entirety or in part, so that if anyone in the group objects to having something he or she has said remain on the cassette, that section can be erased at his or her request and in his or her presence.

4. The taped session will remain confidential—that is, only those people who might normally be permitted to attend a session will be allowed to listen to the cassette, and even then the group will be informed of this in advance so that anyone who wishes to exercise his or her option of having the cassette erased may do so.

5. Explain that during the session, to help keep confidentiality, the group should not use names or anything else that might identify the speaker. The cassette will be played back during each session so the group may audit it.

6. Set up the cassette recorder before the session begins.

7. At the start of the session, demonstrate the use of the cassette recorder to the group. A good way to do this is to record a reiteration of steps 2 through 5. Play this back to the group. This also can act as a test to determine if the machine is working properly.

8. Encourage some group members to record their voices or some informal material such as a song. This informal approach also acts as an icebreaker. Play back this informal session for the group.

9. Ask the group for any reactions or questions they may have about the cassette recorder or its use.

10. Answer all questions fully. Allay any fears that may be observed. Treat the matter informally. Be as encouraging as possible. Demonstrate how erasures can be made.

11. Start the regular part of the session. Be unhurried and relaxed. If the counselor is tense about the process, it will be communicated to the group.

The cassette recorder may be used to record a standard session of group discussion, or it may be used along with special counseling procedures, such as role-taking and role-reversal. At the midpoint of the session, stop to allow time for playback.

It is during the playback section that the cassette recorder demonstrates its greatest usefulness. Invariably, members listen intently to what each of them has said. A keen and sensitive counselor can, through observing the individual reactions of group members, pick

It is during the playback section that the cassette recorder demonstrates its greatest usefulness.

up important clues about what makes some of the members tick. Their reactions are sometimes a dead giveaway.

The intensity with which they audit the cassette can be extreme. At times, it may seem as though they've memorized the session because several of them may accurately anticipate whose voice will be heard next and what will be said. Sometimes during a session, humorous things may have been said and recorded. On the playback, it is rare that the group finds any humor in those same things. They listen with intense seriousness, oblivious to anything but the words being played back.

Sometimes, listening to a playback may motivate a clean-up of language. Some members, testing the freedom of the counseling situation, may have used vulgarity and profanity in their speech. When such sessions are recorded and played back, group members, on hearing themselves using slang or profanity, may become uncomfortable with what they hear. Until then, they may not have had any idea of how they sound to others. When they've heard what they sound like, they can sometimes be their own worst critics. These same people, without the counselor having to say a word of admonition, condemnation, or correction, often clean up their own speech and seldom repeat such language.

This is the beginning of self-discipline—the type of discipline that is not directly imposed by others. It is also an example of the counselor exercising sufficient confidence in the group process to be able to manage it well enough to generate insights and reeducation. In this process, group members are helped not only to act but also to reflect and learn. In this situation, the counselor, instead of being a petty preacher advocating "proper" language, is the enabler who provides the group with an opportunity to hear itself and learn from the experience. This is one way counseling differs from teaching.

Group members tend to listen to the cassette intensely and self-critically. They tend to evaluate what they've said and, with guidance, try to do better. This is the beginning of forethought. Hearing themselves on cassette enables members to get a better glimpse of themselves and what they express. In auditing the taped session individuals may begin to be their own teacher, preacher, and conscience. Of course, this development must be supported and reinforced.

The taped session is an invaluable learning and training device for the counselor. Listening to sessions on cassette may help counselors better evaluate their counseling efforts. They can pick up on their strong points and more easily spot their weak points. They can more clearly study what members have said and pick up on details they might normally have missed. They can be better able to pick up on the important threads of the session and use them to plan future sessions, which, as a result, may be more productively and skillfully conducted. With taped sessions arranged chronologically, the counselor and the group may be in a better position to gauge progress.

The use of videotape follows many of the aforementioned principles. It is advised that the counselor first use the video recorder recreationally, as a fun device. Only when the group becomes very used to it should it be used to tape a session. Always allow time for playback and subsequent discussion of the playback. With videotape, group members can gain many useful insights by seeing and hearing themselves and other group members. Useful provocative questions may be raised by the counselor to stimulate both responses and insight opportunities.

Goal Planning

Goal planning is an especially valuable technique that can be used in a variety of settings and circumstances. It is a technique borrowed from business management, where it is part of a procedure known as management by objective or MBO.

According to MBO procedure, management establishes an objective to be reached or achieved. This may be done by directive or through a process known as "participatory management" in which several levels of management and, in some instances, line personnel become involved in deriving and establishing an agreed-on objective. Once this is done, the next step is to think through each step leading to the ultimate objective. These steps are broken down into sets of tasks needed to complete each step. Each task is then assigned to a specific worker, manager, technician, team, or cluster of teams. Resources, material, space, etc., are also assigned. A time schedule of each of these factors and actions is established, as are time schedules for related actions and contributory factors so that things come together when and where they should.

In MBO, when all of the above are established, a monitoring device lets management know how things are progressing as these events are happening. When zigs or zags occur, management can react immediately rather than wait until deflection increases to the point where a key task cannot be completed or cannot be completed in the time frame that was set, which in turn may mean either late accomplishment of the ultimate objective or failure. This monitoring capability not only allows management to spot deflections and make corrections, it also allows management to reevaluate its established objective and modify or change it.

Some of these notions have been modified and applied to case management. This, in turn, has been applied to group work, of which group counseling is a part. It is important to remember that when this technique borrowed from business/industrial management is applied to people, certain changes in the model are necessary. For example, MBO in business and industry more readily permits measurements to be made. Inputs, such as costs of personnel, materials, space, time, and so forth, can be measured against outputs, such as parts or products produced, sold, and distributed. The subsequent income derived from the output as compared with the investment in input may be expressed as profit.

Management in casework and group work does not involve such easily measured units of input, output, profit, or cost/benefit ratios. In human services, these units are often not as tangible as they would be in business and industry. In human services, results are judged. To do this, the MBO model is applied to counseling; it must be modified so that it considers the human being, with his or her actions and attitudes providing insight that will permit his or her progress—or lack of it—to be monitored in the effort to achieve certain goals and objectives.

In goal planning with a group, the following steps should be followed:

1. Involve group members in selecting goals. Do not select goals for them.

2. The group should agree on the goals selected.

3. Once having selected their goals, group members should accept the responsibility of working toward their achievement.

4. Encourage group members to select small and modest goals at first—realistic goals they can reach.

5. Use the achievement of these small goals as building blocks to the ultimate achievement of larger and more complex goals.

6. Before action is taken, have the group commit itself about what it will do when the goal has been achieved.

7. If staff or others besides group members are needed to contribute to the effort, state what this will be, who will do it and when, and do not promise any input from others that cannot be guaranteed.

8. Have group members set a deadline. If need be, they can change the date, but always have a deadline they are working toward.

The following are steps to take in selecting group goals:

1. Develop a general list of the group's needs—needs that are shared by most if not all group members.

2. Develop a general list of interests of group members—interests shared by most if not all group members.

3. Keep the list of needs and the list of interests separate.

4. Convert these lists into goal statements.

5. Develop a list of group skills, strengths, and abilities.

6. Compare this with the goals.

7. From this comparison, it should be clear when the array of skills, abilities, and strengths are adequate to the probable achievement of some of its goals, which were derived either from the list of needs or the list of interests.

8. Of the goals that seem to be more readily achievable, have the group select some for which there is agreement or consensus as well as an expressed commitment to take sustained and appropriate action within an agreed-on time frame.

9. The goals selected should be stated clearly so that everyone knows exactly what they are, avoiding technical, social work, pseudoclinical, or jargon terms and expressions.

10. Have the group prioritize its goals. Not all goals are equally important, and the early achievement of some goals may make other goals easier to achieve later.

11. Set up, with group participation, a monitoring system that will give the group a clear picture of progress, problems encountered, and help needed.

12. Use group counseling sessions to review progress, problems, issues, and concerns.

13. Use the group process to encourage and support the efforts of each group member or, when appropriate, to constructively pressure noncontributory or unproductive members.

14. As each goal is achieved, move on to others, building on success.

One advantage of group goal planning is that attainments achieved by group effort tend to build a positive sense of group identity—belonging for positive purposes. Group members can derive a sense of accomplishment, the beginnings of mutual trust among some of the members, and for some, the beginning of greater trust in self. A foundation can then be created to develop positive individual self-esteem.

From this point, it becomes easier to augment a process of individual goal planning. This technique is an excellent case management tool. The following steps may be taken:

1. Develop an analysis of client/inmate strengths and needs.

2. Of the needs, set priorities—from most important to the least—based on concerns and issues related to adjustment, readjustment, education, reeducation, ego-support needs, prerelease readiness, work readiness, behavioral change, and so forth.

3. If possible, derive these with the participation of an interdisciplinary team (IDT) composed of the key people working with the individual. In an institutional setting, include representatives of treatment, education, and custody/security.

4. After the derivation of needs priorities by the IDT, involve the client/inmate in the process of goal selection.

5. Goal(s) should be stated in simple terms, be measurable, have a specified start and stop date, and have definite attainment criteria so they will be apparent if and when they are achieved.

6. Progress should be reviewed at regular intervals and goals and/or methodology modified if necessary.

7. Goals should be written in incremental steps, each step small enough for the client/inmate to be able to achieve.

8. Methodology should be tailor-made, e.g., designed to reflect how best to teach the skills to and obtain compliance from the individual.

This is an example of how group and case management can support each other. Again, group counseling is not a substitute for case counseling. Each can and should act in adjunct to the other.

This listing of special methods, techniques, and devices is brief. There are many other good devices that can be profitably used. Some counselors may be particularly inventive and create new and unique devices. When they do, they need to take advantage of the team approach and explore, share, and learn together. Through staff conferences and in-service training, this becomes possible and profitable.

VII. Special Applications

Short-term group counseling may be used to confront issues such as drug and alcohol abuse, AIDS/HIV, prerelease programming, vocational preparation programming, geriatrics programming, and women's issues, to name a few. Counselors competent in any of these areas have acquired knowledge and understanding of each of these issues. They should not be a source of untruths, half-truths, and misinformation, even if it is the result of good intentions.

Fortunately, there are many sources of information on these issues. Federal publications may be obtained from the Government Printing Office. Public and college and university libraries are also great sources; many of them offer a computer search of a wide variety of topics. There are various community-based groups, associations, and organizations that specialize in particular issues. These may be found through the local United Way or the yellow pages. Most such groups are accommodating and will provide basic information.

Counselors cannot perform their duties effectively if they do not have knowledge and understanding of the issues. Counselors can educate themselves or they can learn jointly with the group. It may not be such a bad thing for counselors to admit to the group that they are not sure of the facts and issues and to suggest that the group join them to learn the facts. By doing research with the group, counselors teach group members to get involved and how to go about getting information for themselves.

Vocational Counseling

What a person does for a living is an important part of that person's identity. In times past, a person's occupation was often the source of that person's surname. Some examples are Baker, Carpenter, Tailor, Fletcher (arrow-maker), Smith, Butcher, Farmer, Sailor, Thatcher, Merchant, and Mariner. Having no trade, occupation, or vocation affects a person's self-identity and self-esteem. For some people, even being a criminal is better than being a nobody.

When counseling a group about the world of work, counselors must be familiar with some of the terms and concepts used in vocational counseling. Every profession has some lingo. Vocational counseling is no exception.

Before counselors can recommend a job or an occupation to a person, there is a lot they should know about that person (his or her worker profile) and that job or occupation (its occupational demands). Job matching is a process in which the person's worker profile is matched to the occupational demands of a particular job.

Much of what counselors need to know about a person's worker profile may be found in his or her records. Other information may be gleaned through skillful talks with the person as well as with other staff who have contact with that person. In some instances, tests and evaluations are performed.

Vocational counselors need to know the following:

1. Which work activities does the person prefer? Which does he or she hate?

2. Which work situations does the person prefer? Which does he or she hate?

3. What is the person's general educational development in

   - reasoning?

   - mathematics?

   - language?

4. What is the level of the person's aptitudes in

   - general learning ability?

   - verbal ability?

   - numerical ability?

   - spatial perception (the ability to manipulate space)?

   - form perception?

   - clerical perception?

   - motor coordination?

   - finger dexterity?

   - manual (hand) dexterity?

   - eye-hand-foot coordination?

   - color discrimination?

5. What is the level of the person's physical capacity in

   - lifting, carrying, pushing, pulling?

   - climbing, balancing?

- stooping, kneeling, crouching, crawling?
- reaching, handling, fingering, feeling?
- talking, hearing, seeing?

6. Which working conditions does the person prefers? Which does he or she hate?

7. What is the person's worker function level? (The worker function level is sometimes called DPT because it deals with the level at which a person functions at with data, people, and things.) Each occupation listed in the U.S. Department of Labor's *Dictionary of Occupational Titles* is numbered. The worker function level, or the DPT, is expressed by the middle three digits of the occupation's number. The first number of the three digits expresses the level the job requires for skills with data. The second number expresses the level the job requires for skills with people. The third number expresses the level of skill required for handling things. The smaller the number, the higher the skill level.

Much of this information can be gathered by talking with staff who have had contact with the individual. These may include counselors, social workers, psychologists, teachers, vocational instructors, and correctional officers. The individual to be counseled should also be asked for information. However, if a group is to be counseled, group members should be told what information each person needs to gather so that they may build their own worker profile. Group members should be sent to information sources among the staff (who the counselor has already alerted to expect such requests). The information gathered will render a worker profile. In this way, each person is taught how to develop a database for himself or herself. Once each group member has put together an individual profile, the group should be encouraged to identify jobs that match their profile.

Counselors should then help group members learn how to apply this information to himself or herself. Each group member then participates in the counseling process and becomes a peer counselor for other group members by helping each other through the process.

There are other factors in vocational counseling besides matching skills to job demands and requirements. Some group members may not have a realistic understanding of how the world of work truly functions. Some may be surprised that employers don't think or act like social workers or counselors. Some may be surprised that employers are not necessarily given to understanding the mistakes and delinquencies of employees. Group members need to understand that private industry does not work like a social service agency. Counseling and education or reeducation need to be directed toward helping the person achieve a functional understanding of how to behave on a job, what to expect from employers and from co-workers, how to handle problems on the job, and how to prevent problems.

Group counseling may also address how to conduct a self-directed job search. Group members should not think that finding a job is something others are obligated to do for them while they remain passive and inert.

Another vocational area that can be handled in group counseling is how to keep a job and some of the causes for losing a job (e.g., chronic lateness/absenteeism, friction with other employees/with the boss, theft, and noncompliance with directions).

Money management is a topic that can be included in vocational counseling.

Group members may also be counseled on the unhappiness and frustration they may feel because their educational level may limit their occupational choices to entry-level or "dead-end" jobs. The relationship between education level achieved and occupational opportunity needs to be explored. Having an education will not always guarantee success, but educational achievement *is* likely to provide greater access to opportunity. By teaching group members that many jobs do have a minimum educational requirement for entry, counselors can begin to implant the idea that there is a connection between deficient educational achievement and poverty. One major goal of counseling is to help group members get that point and learn how to change what they've been doing. Getting and keeping a job is a good place to start.

Money management is another topic that can be included in vocational counseling. Many people have jobs but cannot manage their paychecks.

Putting together a resume, applying for an interview, preparing and taking part in an interview, using the phone to inquire about employment, and reading and interpreting help wanted ads are just a few additional topics group counseling can cover. Some ways to get discussion started might include presenting some provoking hypothetical incidents. Some examples of hypothetical incidents counselors may propose are as follows:

1. Suppose you were on your way to your first day on the job. You are riding to work on a bus. Somebody gets on the bus with a cup of coffee and stands next to your seat. The bus lurches, and coffee spills all over you. You are thirty minutes from home, ten minutes from your next job. What would you do?

2. Suppose you've been working on the job for a few months as an assistant to a drill press operator. One morning the boss comes up to you and says, "The porter is out sick today. The bathrooms are a mess. I'd like you to clean them up." What would you do?

Counselors may make up other reaction-provoking situations to present to the group. They should help group members track down the probable consequences of each suggested "solution" so that they learn the probable consequences of some of their behavior. By learning what effects can grow out of some of their traditional behavior, they can be taught to look for better ways to deal with provocation and problems.

Many times, people can prepare to handle emergencies by practicing responses to provoking situations. Like the example in Chapter III of pilot trainees using computer-programmed simulators to test their responses to various emergencies that can come up in real flight, group members who practice responding to provoking situations can learn to be more effective and constructive.

Stress Counseling

Many inmates have difficulty dealing with incarceration. Counselors should approach this situation from the beginning, before it generates more problems.

There are many circumstances and conditions within an institutional setting that can produce stress for the inmate population and for staff. Inmates affected by unrelieved stress are unlikely to benefit fully from

When attempting to deal with stress, it is important to deal with the entire person, body and soul.

correctional programs and services. Stress lowers energy reserves. It takes energy to cope with life in prison. Offenders should not be released into the community angrier, more hostile, more embittered, and more antisocial than they were when they were first incarcerated. Staff may also be susceptible to the negative effects of stress. So it is in the staff's best interest to help inmates deal with stress and to not support stress-producing circumstances.

Because there are physical, emotional, and medical aspects to stress, it should not to be treated through counseling alone, be it group or individual. Stress can affect the heart, the digestive system, and the circulatory system. It can be a cause of cardiovascular disease, heart attack, stroke, and, some scientists suspect, some forms of cancer. When attempting to deal with stress, it is important to deal with the entire person, body and soul. Therefore, short-term group counselors should be joined by other staff in an effort to address all of the factors that are or can be affected by stress.

Counseling cannot take the place of other services, but it does have a place and a role in the treatment of stress overload or stress prevention. If group counseling is used to educate, sessions should be planned to help group members learn what stress is and what its symptoms are. There are many good and basic source books, some of which may be obtained from the government through the Government Printing Office. The local Heart Association is another possible source of basic information on stress and how to handle it. Institutional medical and nursing services may also help counselors build an information base as well as help deliver some educational programs.

Group counseling may also serve to reeducate by helping group members identify the things they are either doing or not doing that contribute to the generation of stress. Once these are identified, group members may be taught more effective ways to avoid stress, cope with it, and relieve some of it. After group members learn which behaviors harm them and which behaviors can reduce or control the problem, sessions may be used to encourage group members to put what they have learned into practice. Role-playing, role-reversals, audio-visual aids, and discussion are but a few of the techniques that can be used successfully.

In helping group members learn how to better cope, short-term group counseling combines educational and reeducational techniques with moral support. This is often referred to as "ego-supportive" counseling. It is often difficult to give up old ways for new ways, even when the old ways have always involved trouble and hurting oneself and others. It takes courage and effort to learn and adopt new and unfamiliar behavior that initially seems threatening and suspect. Counselors who have the trust of group members should indicate that they will stand by each person who tries the new and gives up the old.

Group members who feel that the strength and integrity of the counselor will defend, help, and protect them are apt to be more willing to try. As modest success builds on modest success, counselors should slowly withdraw supports until the individual can function independently.

"Modest success" is a key concept. Counselors should have a plan in which development goals and objectives to be achieved are listed in steps small enough to ensure success but large enough to challenge the individual. Challenge and achievement spur human growth and development. Supportive counseling provides group members a sense of protection and security that enables some of them to take on risks they might otherwise never have taken on by themselves.

Group counselors should remain intensively involved with all the members of the interdisciplinary team. In this way, the delivery of services can be coordinated while each professional strengthens the contributions of the others.

AIDS and HIV Counseling

Many people are frightened of individuals who have human immunodeficiency virus (HIV) or who have acquired immune deficiency syndrome (AIDS). AIDS is a dreadful and deadly illness. No race or gender is immune. It can strike heterosexuals as well as homosexuals. In can strike the rich as well as the poor, the city dweller as well as the suburbanite as well as the rural person. It can strike the educated as well as the illiterate.

It is transmitted by sexual intercourse or through infected needles shared by intravenous drug users. It can be transmitted when the blood of an individual with HIV invades a cut, wound, or sore of another person. Mothers who are HIV-positive can transmit it to their infants through breastfeeding. An embryo can be infected in its mother's uterus if its mother has HIV.

The Centers for Disease Control, in Atlanta, Georgia, is one of the main sources for information on HIV and AIDS. There are also training programs available for those interested in counseling individuals who have HIV or AIDS.

Here is some basic information:

1. The human body has an immune system that fights infections. The immune system of individuals with AIDS is so damaged that it becomes less and less able to fight infec-

tions that have invaded the body. When the immune system is no longer able to fight off infections, the individual dies.

2. HIV eventually breaks down the body's immune system, resulting in AIDS. Individuals at high risk of getting AIDS fall into one or more of the following groups:

   - homosexual men

   - bisexual men

   - intravenous drug users

   - babies born to infected mothers

   - sexual partners of individuals with AIDS or of individuals in one of the high-risk groups

   - individuals who used blood products between 1977 and 1985 (a period when blood products were not properly screened)

3. AIDS is transmitted when the blood, semen, or vaginal fluid of an infected person is passed into another person's blood by sharing needles, through sexual intercourse, or through open sores or wounds. Babies can be infected through the blood of the mother passing through the umbilical cord or through the mother's milk when breastfed if the mother, herself, has been infected.

4. AIDS is not transmitted by simply sharing close quarters with an infected individual. It is not transmitted by hugging or touching an individual with AIDS; it is not transmitted by using the telephone, sitting on toilet seats, coughing, sneezing, being bitten by mosquitos, donating blood, or eating food that was prepared by an individual with AIDS.

5. Some of the symptoms of AIDS include unexplained weight loss; fatigue; fever lasting more than two weeks; swollen glands in the neck, armpits, or groin; white spots in the mouth or on the tongue; persistent diarrhea; night sweats; flu-like symptoms; and dark spots on the skin. There are, however, many individuals who are infected but who don't show symptoms. It is possible that, even though these individuals show no symptoms, they can still infect others. It may take up to ten years for a person who has contracted HIV to develop AIDS.

6. All employees of correctional facilities should learn their facility's policies and procedures concerning standard

practices for avoiding infection of HIV, AIDS, and other contagious diseases. Medical staff may also be able to offer information on antiseptic procedures to avoid infection.

Counseling individuals with HIV or AIDS, either individually or in groups, requires counselors to become familiar with the disease and the infectious process, step-by-step. As the infected individual goes through the various phases and steps, the goals and objectives of counseling must be modified. For example, the approach used to counsel an individual who has just been found to be HIV-positive can be quite different from the approach used to counsel an individual who is suffering through the last stages of AIDS. Here, too, the counselor must work not as an individual, but as a member of the interdisciplinary team assigned to the person.

The increase in the number of HIV-positive individuals in the general population is reflected in the corrections population. Those who work in the correctional system will encounter individuals infected with HIV and AIDS. These individuals should be treated with compassion and courtesy; there is no need to hate, fear, or scorn them.

Two major issues to be approached in group counseling those who are infected with HIV or AIDS are (1) how each group member can use the rest of his or her life and (2) how to confront death.

AIDS is seen as a terminal illness. This means that counseling content and processes must ultimately confront issues related to death and dying. In *Living with Death and Dying*, psychiatrist Elizabeth Kubler-Ross describes five stages through which a dying person passes:

- shock and denial
- anger
- bargaining
- depression
- acceptance

These are psychological stages and, as such, have great meaning for those who deliver counseling to individuals with AIDS. These stages do not necessarily happen in the order in which they are listed here. It is possible that some stages may recycle, sometimes several times. It is also possible for an individual to experience more than one stage at a time.

The shock and denial stage can happen at any time: at the first signs of illness, at the time of diagnosis, or at the time of being told that AIDS is incurable and fatal. Individuals may say, "This can't be true" or "There must be some mistake" or "It's only a cold" or "A cure is sure to be found any day now." Sometimes, denial is a necessary and helpful way for individuals to cope. Take this away from some people, and they can break down. In counseling, it is often unwise to strip a person's defenses without putting something else in place that is equal to or better than the defenses that were taken away. Only in cases where denial is very likely to have destructive effects is it appropriate to neutralize denial behavior.

In the anger stage, individuals are likely to ask, "Why me? Why not you? Why not anybody else?" They feel bitter and resentful. The anger can be directed toward God, doctors, or just about anyone who is around—even loved ones. It is very important for individuals to vent that anger, to express it. If suppressed, anger toward other individuals or toward things can turn against self and may result in suicide. To help individuals in the anger stage, counselors should be willing to listen to them and encourage them to express their feelings.

The bargaining stage is marked by the individual wishing to "live until my next birthday" or "live until next Christmas" and offering trades with God, for example, promising certain things in exchange for granting the wish. These individuals feel that, if only the final event can be postponed a bit, they may be better able to cope with the situation later. This, too, may be a necessary defense—without it, the individual may be extremely vulnerable.

Depression usually follows when individuals finally accept enough of the truth that a sense of reality grows. Most individuals become very sad and melancholy when they realize they are dying. The speed and depth of depression varies from person to person and, even within the same person, from moment to moment. It is usually not a very stable stage. Some individuals, especially those who harbor suicidal tendencies or death wishes, might actually experience a sense bordering on the happy or manic or a sense of relief, while others may bounce back and forth from manic to depressive.

The stage of acceptance is reached when individuals come to terms with what is happening and will likely happen. Some people may never reach this stage.

Counseling can play a major role in each of these stages. At any point, group members will need supportive counseling, with the degree and frequency varying from time to time and from person to person. Some will have a painless death. Others will die painfully. Much depends on what illness attacks them. Individuals with AIDS don't die of AIDS per se, but rather AIDS weakens the immune system to the point where the individual is susceptible to a variety of infections. They die as a result of these infections and illnesses.

AIDS counseling is not just for those who are HIV-positive. Remember that many inmates practice a lifestyle that places them within the at-risk population. Group counseling, in its educative and reeducative functions, can be used to deliver information on HIV and AIDS, with special emphasis on safe sexual practices.

Individuals who have HIV and those who have AIDS have many problems beyond the medical. There are social problems that become evident when they are socially isolated because other people are afraid to be near them. They may be vocationally isolated because many fear to work with them. They may be scorned and hated as well. If the individual has family, what to tell them (if they don't already know) can present a mountain of problems. If the inmate is scheduled for release, where can he or she obtain treatment, an apartment, a job? Counselors should help set up a support system and have it in place before the inmate is released. If the counselor is part of an interdisciplinary team managing the inmate's case, a plan needs to be created, with the informed consent of the inmate, goals and objectives set forth, time tables established, and monitoring mechanisms put in place. The group counselor is a key participant in this process when the effort moves from treating individuals to treating groups.

Counselors have several sources of information, including the following:

- AIDS Action Council, 729 Eighth St., Washington, DC 20003; 202/547-3101

- AIDS Hotline (Centers of Disease Control); 800/342-AIDS

- American Red Cross AIDS Education Office, 1730 D St., Washington, DC 20006; 202/737-8300

- Gay Men's Health Crisis, 132 W. 24th St., New York City, NY 10011; 212/807-6664

- Hispanic AIDS Forum, 140 W. 22 St. New York City, NY 10011; 212/463-8264

- National AIDS Network, 2033 M St., N.W., Suite 800, Washington, DC 20036; 202/293-2437

- U.S. Public Health Service, Room 721-H, Humphry Bldg., 2000 Independence Ave., S.W., Washington, DC 20201; 202/245-6867

Local sources, particularly the local department of health, also offer basic information on HIV and AIDS. The institutional medical staff may also prove helpful to counselors, not only in giving them information, but also in helping them to interpret the information they already possess.

Drug and Alcohol Abuse

If an individual wants to play the role of a father or of a mother, that individual will not be able to do so unless someone else agrees to play the role of son or daughter. In effect, almost every role requires that it be interfaced with a role that both complements and supports it. This is no less true of those who are addicts. To play the part of the addict or abuser, other people have to play the complementary and supportive roles that make the role of addict or abuser possible—either by what he or she did or did not do, or both.

Although drug abusers must be held accountable for their actions, they didn't get to be what they are by themselves. Effective counseling of drug abusers must address the influences and behavior of those who played roles in creating the current condition or circumstance.

When I was director of Pennsylvania's first diagnostic and classification center for juvenile offenders, one young boy in the population was exceptionally overweight and had been diagnosed as having severe diabetes. When his mother came to visit him, she brought with her a large shopping bag. The bag was searched and was found to contain several pounds of candies and other sweets. (The boy was being held at the center for a burglary he had committed to obtain funds to buy sweets.) This situation made me aware of the connection between the abuser's predicament and the actions of those who supported the abuse, by commission or omission.

Why would a person aid, abet, and encourage another person's self-destructive actions and behavior? Most of those who do this know the potentially lethal outcome, either consciously or unconsciously. This phenomenon is called "codependency."

Counselors need to take a closer look at drug abuse to better understand it. All drugs are not alike. Some energize those who use them. But sometimes, these drugs have the opposite effect, and the user experiences a depressive reaction. It is clear that the effects of these drugs are not always as predicted.

Some drugs give users a sense of well-being, a feeling that all is well and wonderful, even when, in reality, the opposite is true. These drugs distort reality and impair judgment.

How much of the drug must a person take before becoming addicted? This varies from person to person according to the drug, the person's psychological status, the person's weight, the amount and frequency of use, and other factors, including the person's metabolic rate and the condition of the person's liver and other organs. Abusing drugs is similar to playing Russian Roulette where the gun has several loaded chambers—there is a high risk of becoming addicted.

Matters become more complicated in cases where several kinds of drugs are used. Drugs may interact with each other. A drug that is harmless by itself can become deadly when combined with another drug. Many drugs, such as barbiturates, should not be taken with alcohol because the mixture can have a deadly outcome.

Substance abuse counselors need to be informed about the nature of abused substances and their physical and mental effects on the abuser. For example, a substance abuser with a badly damaged liver can present special problems that need to be addressed by all members of the interdisciplinary team—medical, psychological, social, vocational, and so forth. This would also be true for abusers who experience flashbacks, where the abuser starts to act and feel as though under the influence of the substance weeks, months, or even years after he or she used that substance. Some drugs give users a high, some produce depression, and others generate hallucinations—visual, auditory, or kinesthetic (feeling things). Counselors must know enough about the drugs to be able to get a handle on what is happening to the substance abuser and why.

Substance abuse often leads to addiction. This is a condition where the individual's physical and mental state have become so unstable that a marked dependency on the substance has developed. Withdrawal from the substance may produce painful and distressful reactions. In its most severe form, withdrawal can kill.

Most professionals feel that it is a waste of time to counsel anyone who has not reached the point where the residue of the substance has been metabolized or leached from the body—detoxified.

Should group counselors put together a group composed only of persons who are recovering abusers or should a mixed group be formed that includes abusers as well as those who have never abused substances but who have a number of problems in common with those who have?

There are those who say that isolating recovering abusers by keeping them in the exclusive company of each other permits a depth of interaction that is greater because the participants share a common experience. Others claim that a group composed only of those who have abused substances reinforces the deviance of each person in the group.

If, during a group session composed entirely of recovering substance abusers, there is movement in the group process where members begin to reinforce each other's deviances, the counselor should be competent enough to know how to redirect the session or, if necessary, terminate it.

In group sessions, counselors should help group members identify what brought them to substance abuse—how they got to that condition. They need to be helped to gain insight into their own role, responsibility, and accountability. They need help to discover alternate ways of responding when again faced with these pressures, temptations, needs, and cravings. They need help to understand that they are not alone. They also need to learn how and where to find help and support in the effort to avoid substance abuse. When leaving the institution, recovering addicts should be referred to community-based support groups, with appropriate institutional staff acting as the bridge to the community-based support groups.

One important task for a counselor to obtain is an understanding of how the world looks from the shoes of group members.

Women's Issues

At one time, the issues presented by the incarceration of women were not recognized or, if recognized, were seldom given the attention they deserved. A female inmate is not merely a feminine version of a male inmate. To treat men and women the same way is not equal treatment for women because women do not necessarily have the same needs that men do.

Although there is much that men and women share with each other, there remains a great deal that is gender-specific in the way each is taught to think, feel, and act. Counselors need to confront and understand stereotypes based on gender and to ensure that these stereotypes do not affect the way group counseling is conducted.

One way group counselors can become better informed is to set up a series of sessions in which groups of women are encouraged to identify and discuss these issues, their feelings about these issues, and recommendations as to what might be done about them. Counselors can help these women explore their feelings:

1. How do they feel about their current predicament and circumstance?

2. How do they feel about the conditions that brought them to this state of affairs?

3. How do they feel about treatment they have been given?

4. What's missing from their daily lives that is especially important to them as women?

5. What do they see their future to be?

In effect, counselors help group members articulate how the world looks to them: in the past, the present, and the future.

One important task for any group counselor is to obtain a functional understanding of how the world looks from the shoes of group members. Counselors must be able to discern which of these views are skewed or defective from those that are reality-based. Group counseling should be directed toward helping group members become better able to make such distinctions for themselves.

Once group members are able to do this more effectively, they need to be helped to learn how to handle not only the realities but also the unrealities. Counselors should remember that what an individual believes to be true *is* true for that individual. People act not on what is true but, rather, on what they believe is true. If one's beliefs generate a major portion of one's life's problems, these beliefs need to be examined. Group counseling is a good vehicle to conduct this examination.

Group counseling also provides feedback. Sensitive issues uncovered or discovered in group sessions can be brought to the attention of the interdisciplinary treatment team to help sensitize the team to needs that may have gone unrecognized or underprioritized to date. Pertinent information should also be shared with custody and security staff and management and administration. Counselors should assure group members that they will use information members share with them only for positive purposes designed to help the members, thereby establishing the parameters for confidentiality.

Prerelease Counseling

When an inmate serves the required time, he or she may be discharged with no special preparation. This individual may not be prepared to adjust to life on the outside and may soon find himself or herself in trouble with the law once again. For those employed in the system, adjusting to the outside after one's shift is over is not always easy. Imagine what it may be like for someone who has been confined as an inmate for months and years.

Group counseling can be used to prepare inmates to cope with their return to the community. Inmates about to be released should learn how to deal with making choices and how to cope effectively with pressures and stresses. They should develop the physical and emotional stamina required to hold down a job. They need to learn the basics about managing time and money, budgeting, paying bills, establishing and maintaining social relationships, using leisure time, and finding a place to live.

These issues can be frightening and stressful to someone who has been incarcerated. For example, if a newly released man is uncertain of his ability to perform adequately sexually, he may feel anxiety and stress when confronted by a compliant wife or girlfriend who is sexually assertive to him. This situation may sound better in fantasy than it is in real life. Newly released individuals need time to adjust to the outside. They need to adjust in their own time at their own pace.

By projecting the circumstances, feelings, and needs that a newly released individual is likely to face, group counseling sessions can educate and reeducate the individual to better cope.

Group discussions may be coupled with role-taking, role-reversal, audio-visual aids, and guest speakers, such as representatives from the labor department or employment agencies, potential employers, human sexuality counselors, social workers, and school representatives.

Sessions that include family members can help prepare offenders emotionally and informationally to be a functioning part of the family when released. Such sessions may include families of several group members, or a special session may be arranged for a particular group member and his or her family, as a family unit.

In involving the family, counselors may open session attendance to any family member or may limit attendance to those who appear to be of greatest significance. Significant others may be a source of support—an adjunct to the interdisciplinary support team.

If the former inmate is to be supervised by a parole agent, that agent should be invited to become involved in this process early on. The agent is a logical bridge to the community and to community-based services and can pick up on service deliveries where institutional services leave off.

Shared-interest Counseling

Short-term group counseling may be used to help reduce or to stop disputes between groups. At times, these disputes can develop into major incidents unless they are defused.

The process of shared-interest counseling can be used to help opposing groups identify shared needs, interests, investments, and conditions. Once this is done, the counselor helps the groups discover that each not only has some power to hurt the other but also, in the process, will injure some of its own interests, needs, values, investments, and conditions. It's like helping each side understand that they share the same boat and it's silly to think that they can sink the other guys' side of the boat without sinking their own.

In effect, the counselor becomes an "honest broker," negotiating between opposing groups. However, to be accepted in that role, the counselor must be perceived to be impartial, unbiased, and trustworthy. Correctional officers who are also counselors may find that it takes time for group members to learn to trust them enough to allow them to take the role of middleman, honest broker, or evenhanded negotiator.

This is why only those staff who enjoy such a reputation should attempt shared-interest counseling. Counselors using shared-interest counseling must be well-balanced and have control over emotional and internal stress. They must have a clear sense of their limits and authority.

Shared-interest counseling requires participants to engage in some give and take. Group members who have leadership roles over other members have to be very careful about give and take because they cannot risk being seen as weak or weaker than opposing leaders during the negotiation process. Compromise becomes risky and can become dangerous if it is not carefully overseen by counselors. Counselors must set up conditions that can make it easier for give and take to occur.

One way to bring this about is to structure and guide the process toward a solution in which everyone gains—where there is something in it for everybody. This is sometimes referred to as a "win/win" outcome. This is very important in a setting where no one, especially the leader, can be seen as backing down. To accomplish this, the atmosphere must be one of trades, not concessions.

Five basic methods are traditionally used to handle conflicts:

- competition
- collaboration
- compromise
- avoidance
- accommodation

Each of these methods has both advantages and disadvantages.

Competition

Advantages of competition are as follows:

1. Competing can be useful when a quick outcome of almost any kind is needed, when delays can be too costly or dangerous, or when even a "bad" or undesirable outcome is better than prolonging the situation. A hard-fought and quick competition can be a useful strategy, especially if the power, influence, and resources to obtain a favorable decision or outcome are present.

2. Some people will compete whether the other side is willing or not. They will take advantage of the other side's unwillingness to compete or may view the other side's offer to compromise as evidence of weakness and a lack of both will and courage. In such a case, competition is difficult to avoid.

Competition has several disadvantages:

1. It stops the process of examining other options and approaches.

2. It confines choices to only those who are directly involved in the competition.

3. One side can win only at the expense of the other; it's all or nothing, a win/lose situation.

4. Power and skill count for more than ethics, morality, or rights.

5. It brings about a temporary solution because the problem is still there.

Collaboration

Advantages of collaboration include the following:

1. Through collaboration, both sides can explore creative options and possible solutions together.

2. Conflict can be resolved through consensus—mutual agreement.

3. There are no losers: all who participate are winners, a win/win situation.

4. Each participant is committed to supporting the mutual agreements or risks being seen as a breakaway from the groups(s), a loner.

5. The outcome is likely to be long-lasting.

Disadvantages include the following:

1. It may take a lot of time for participants to work out their differences.

2. All who are involved need to participate fully. A lowered level of participation by any person(s) can lower the level of commitment to the agreement or even lower the chances of arriving at an agreement.

Compromise

Compromise means making some concessions; it can also involve trade offs or exchanges. This idea of trade offs is used in shared-interest counseling to make it easier for participants to avoid the appearance of giving in. Rather than appear to have given in, they appear to just "make trades."

Some advantages of compromise include the following:

1. Each side can win some of the things it wants, so all can claim a "victory."
2. Total loss is avoided by all. Nobody loses everything.
3. The level of risk is reduced for all participants.
4. Because everyone gets something out of the deal, the risk of anyone creating a long-term blockage of action is reduced.
5. The agreements and trade offs create boundaries and limits, thereby establishing and improving on a sense of security for all.

Some of the disadvantages are as follows:

1. One side or the other may have to trade off something they want or need very much to obtain something else they want or need.
2. If one side is not as gifted in trading as the other side, it can lose more than the other side (or win less).
3. The trade off one side makes may later prove to be far less satisfying or valuable as it had first been thought, and as such, the agreement can fall apart later.
4. If those who negotiate do not have the authority to make the deal they made, those who do have the power may refuse to accept the agreement or support the negotiator(s) who made it.
5. It is possible that the deal that was made is no better or even worse than could have been made with the use of power, force, pressure, superior resources, or just plain toughness.

Avoidance

Avoidance is a strategy for getting out of a possible conflict by not getting into one at all. Some advantages of avoidance are as follows:

1. If the situation is risky—to the point where the cost of risk is far greater than the benefits that can be gained—it is probably better to avoid the situation. One of the best avoidance tactics is *preventive* action. This may include timely intervention to keep the situation from reaching a critical point, or it may include planned nonintervention to allow things to calm down when intervention may have a negative effect.

2. If facing the conflict can cause an unacceptable increase in stress levels, then avoiding the conflict is another way of avoiding stress. (However, some people are more likely to experience an increase in stress levels if asked to avoid conflict than they would be if asked to enter it. Such individuals include those who see avoidance as being cowardly or as a betrayal and are not able to tolerate this emotionally. This is yet another reason why it is important for counselors to really know the group(s) well before selecting or recommending a strategy for resolving conflicts.)

3. Avoidance can buy time for the building of assets, strengths, and supports needed for success when switching to a strategy more likely to produce success.

4. It can buy time needed for people to cool down.

5. It allows more time to permit the entry of others who are more skilled or powerful enough to deal more effectively with trade offs than those now engaged.

Disadvantages are as follows:

1. Input and contribution of individuals cannot take place because avoidance deprives opportunity for input.

2. The solution is usually temporary. The conflict or its alternative issue will likely catch fire again because nothing had been resolved.

3. Not to decide is, of itself, a kind of decision; avoidance may fall into this category.

4. Avoidance may be seen by some as a kind of weakness and, as such, may encourage others to offer a challenge or opposition.

Accommodation

Accommodation is a flexible and nonhardline approach in which one side gives priority to the demands, wishes, views, and needs of the other side over those of its own side. Advantages are as follows:

1. It can preserve harmony.

2. It can limit or avoid disruptions and turbulence.

3. If the issues are not important to one side, they can give them away to the other side in exchange for later favors. These may be of equal or greater value than those that had been surrendered earlier.

4. Accommodation may prevent or put limits on competition— this is a good thing if competition can produce a negative or undesirable outcome.

Disadvantages include the following:

1. The possibility of putting together a creative resolution is killed off by the "giveaway."

2. One side's point of view, needs, and wishes are sacrificed in favor of those of the other side.

3. Another chance to affect the outcome may not come again.

4. One side wins, and the other side loses.

Selecting a Strategy

When selecting a strategy from the ones mentioned, a balance sheet with positives on one side and negatives on the other may help. This should be done for each option. Each option can then by evaluated as to its benefits, costs, positives, negatives, and general feasibility.

Problem Solving

Short-term group counseling may be used to educate or reeducate the group on matters concerning problem solving. The following is a step-by-step process for resolving problems and conflicts that may be taught to group members:

1. Determine if the problem affects you alone or others as well.

2. If it affects you, decide if you want to go ahead on your own or if you should involve others to get help.

3. If you want or need to involve others, determine who they should be and what role you want them to play. Recruit them. Orient them.

4. If the problem(s) or conflict(s) affects others, involve them in the effort to resolve the matter(s).

5. Define the problem/conflict, and express it in clear and simple terms.

6. Define the outcome you wish/prefer.

7. Obtain the consensus of others who are involved in setting forth the goals and objectives.

8. List all the possible action steps and alternatives for each desired goal and objective.

9. For each action step/option, predict the possible outcome(s) and impact(s).

10. Decide which steps are best by evaluating for each of the following:

    • probable outcome(s) and impact(s)

    • reality (Can you carry it out? Do you have the power, authority, resources, and backup?)

    • timeliness (Is the problem time-sensitive, and if so, does the plan respect this?)

    • results (Do the action steps address the problem fully?)

11. Develop an action plan.

12. Assign roles, duties, and tasks to each participant.

13. Assign the order of action steps—what comes first, second, third, etc.

14. State the criteria of success for each step (what each step must achieve, at a minimum).

15. Evaluate outcomes at each step, and use this information to steer these steps, amending the plan of action as or if necessary.

16. If the goal is not achieved, modify it to a more modest degree, level, or range that can be more readily achieved. On

the other hand, if the goal is too easily achieved, modify it more ambitiously.

Counselors should involve the group in a technique called "brainstorming." Brainstorming increases the quality and quantity of ideas by involving group members in the process. Some ground rules should be observed when carrying out a brainstorming session with a group. Among these ground rules are the following:

1. All ideas are to be freely expressed, with no censorship, criticism, or evaluation by anyone.

2. All ideas are to be listed, with no exception.

3. Ideas are not to be discussed during the idea-generation phase because even a bad or incomplete idea can stimulate the generation of another idea that may turn out to be a gem.

4. Nothing should be done to stifle the generation and flow of ideas. When criticism or premature comments are permitted, unusual or creative ideas can be discouraged or killed.

5. Only when ideas stop flowing does the group turn to look at what has been generated and begin the process of sorting out the ideas listed, weighing each idea for timeliness, practicality, reality, and potential affect on resolving the conflict.

Out of this effort, an action plan can be produced. Of course, it won't help to have a plan if it isn't carried out. The counselor must help the group go from planning to acting.

The process of shared-interest counseling, with some changes, can be applied to working with inmate groups that are in conflict with each other, to staff groups at odds with each other (e.g., when a conflict exists among shifts or when it exists between custody staff and treatment staff), and also in cases where inmates and staff are in conflict with each other (e.g., from a disturbance to hostage negotiation to negotiation over prison conditions).

If the process needs to be applied to a conflict condition between inmates and staff (or administration), staff should go through the problem-solving process. Doing so will allow staff to develop a set of agreed-on issues, goals, objectives and action steps among themselves. Only when this is done are negotiators prepared to take on an adversarial inmate group.

When approaching a contentious group, it is important to note who speaks for them. Some who claim this distinction are self-appointed. Some may have been picked by their peers to speak for them. It should be clear that the staff team would be at a disadvantage if it did not know who holds the strings of real power on the other side.

There have been occasions when the initial inmate negotiators were not the real power holders, but were "fronting" for the real leaders, testing the situation and taking the risks for them. If and when it looks like a real negotiation is to take place, the real leaders may step forward to complete the negotiations and take the credit among their peers. As it is in the game of golf, golfers play the ball where it lies: begin with what you've got.

During the talks, staff negotiators should keep seeking out who really speaks for the inmates. During this phase, it is important not to say or do anything that would worsen the situation. Negotiators should be calm, firm, simple, and straightforward. They should not rise to the bait of provocation, no matter how extreme the provocation may be. They need to keep in mind that it is important to get a complete inventory of what the other side wants; if this is not done, the list will grow without end.

Staff negotiators should have a list of what they, as negotiators, want, need, and demand. Staff negotiators should also know which of these items cannot be traded-off under any circumstance. Of the items that *can* be traded-off, it must be decided what will be demanded in exchange, how much of this for how much of that, and what must be all or nothing.

In cases where the conflict is between the institution and its inmates, the ground rules, needs, and requirements of both the institution and the system should prevail over those of any staff person unless the institution or the system waives its priorities in favor of the interests of the person involved.

In conducting shared-interest counseling between groups in conflict, it is important to not only get each side to list its grievances, complaints, and irritations, which counselors should treat seriously, but to also compare the lists. In many cases, there are a lot of similarities between the two lists. Each side should exchange lists with the other. Each side, *in private*, should then be given a chance to read through, discuss, and think about the other side's list. Each side should then be asked to prepare a response, point by point, that is to be presented to the other side.

Next it must be decided who is to be present when the two sides get together for the purpose of delivering their responses to the other side. Within each group there are likely to be some individuals who can do a better job than those who have assumed leadership roles. There is also the possibility that one or more of the groups' leaders (in the case of inmate groups) may not be emotionally stable. What should the counselor do then?

One option is to convince each side to permit the counselor to deliver its response to the other side, in the presence of both groups. However, this cannot happen unless the counselor has already established a sense of trust with both groups. Once the groups agree to this, the counselor must be especially scrupulous in presenting each side's response with absolute accuracy and absolutely no distortion.

At this point, the counselor may, with group input, develop a list of interests each side shares with the other. The groups can then pick out which of these shared interests will be damaged if agreement is not reached.

The groups should then determine what is more important and valuable to each side: winning as many points as they can, even at the expense of some of their shared interests, or agreeing that some of these shared interests are more valuable than some of the points they have raised.

When the groups permit some flexibility to enter into their demands, trade offs can be discussed. It is important that trade offs *not* be given the character of win/lose but, rather, how each side can win something.

In this, counselors can play key roles in setting up the "atmosphere" in which each side is willing to trade for what it wants from the other. Also, each demand must be assigned a value level and placed on a hierarchy of the most important to the least important. This helps each side get a sense of what is worth trading for what. It may be a one-for-one trade or two-for-one, etc., depending on the value placed on each item and its place in the hierarchy of all items. Each group must decide its own values to be placed on each of the items on its list. In the process of negotiation, values may need to be changed. The groups should be given the chance to do so, in private, when necessary.

After the "easy" items are dealt with by trade offs, what is left is usually the hard core, the nucleus, of the differences between the two groups. These differences have some bases—they were not created out of thin air. It may be necessary to talk more about how these conflicts and differences came about than about what they are. It may be that nobody can even remember how it all started. For example, some street gangs have been fighting each other for generations. In some cases, gang members do not know how it all began. They accept what is, without much thought as to how it got that way. Similar situations can be found in institutions.

The counselor may need to help the groups peel the conflict back, layer by layer, to the earliest point that can be reconstructed. This should be done with each group separately because the process calls for dredging up old grievances, some of which are still very provocative. When counseling each group to help group members get at the origins of their disputes, the counselor should *never* carry tales from one group to the other. To do so would be a gross breach of professionalism—and very dangerous. The counselor's ability to observe confidentiality will add to his or her reputation for trustworthiness.

If these steps have been successful, the counselor may then go on to the next step. However, if any previous step has not been successful, the counselor is advised to carefully review the process, methods, and techniques used and to modify them before proceeding.

It may be necessary for counselors to obtain help and/or information from others that can provide new insight on how to proceed. This is where good relations with colleagues pay off. Others may know something about the dispute between the groups or about some of the group members that the counselor does not. Case records should be reexamined with far greater depth than before and a better database should be established. Then, plan again and, after planning, execute the plan.

Counselors should ask each side separately to list the issues that remain unresolved, starting with the most important to the least important. The origins of these issues should be discussed with each group separately. Counselors should find out from each group what it would take to eliminate the issue or, failing that, reduce it. This information should be carried back to the other side and discussed with them, probing for evidence of slack and flexibility that could then be used in the process of breaking the gridlock. Counselors may need to go back and forth many times, but they should keep chipping away and not allow positions to harden. If they do, it becomes very difficult to soften them enough to obtain further movement forward.

The counselor repeats this process until enough of the issues have been resolved to make each side feel that they are accomplishing something.

Effective counselors will use time to help soften positions that seem rigid and inflexible. One technique is to keep negotiations going until some of the group begin to tire. If used correctly, this can work in favor of a successful outcome. Resistance can sometimes soften when the holdouts get very tired.

Time can also be used to give people more of an opportunity to review their position. If, during that time, counselors can help group members reflect on what they stand to gain and stand to lose, it may be possible to reduce resistance if they can be shown that they stand to gain more and to lose less by cutting a deal now rather than later—especially if delays in reaching an agreement will further inflame participants. Counselors can help group members make a wiser choice than they could likely have made on their own.

Once some acceptable trade offs have been made and agreements have been reached, counselors should write them down. Each group should be given a copy, in separate sessions held for each side. Counselors should ask for comments on accuracy but should avoid having any side amend the substance of the agreement. If this happens, the process will have to start all over again.

A final copy of the agreement should then be given to all concerned. If, in the future, any member wants to question or challenge the agreement's contents, the final copy may be used as a reference point in discussions that come out of this challenge. The agreement may be amended if both sides discuss and agree to the amendment. Those who break the agreement can be confronted with it and asked to conform. As the penalty for nonconformance, this person's word would not to be trusted in any future negotiation, should one take place. The counselor, on that basis, may choose to exclude such persons and explain to the other participants why. This would reinforce to others the importance of keeping one's word.

Inmates who are emotionally ill, violent, or severely unstable need to be treated clinically; they should not be included in shared-interest counseling unless they have a demonstrated capacity to profit from participation and to participate in such a way that is not disruptive. This is true of almost any program. No one should be allowed to participate at the expense of others.

If, during shared-interest counseling, the counselor is asked to make commitments on behalf of the institution or the system, the counselor is well advised not to do so. Counselors usually do not have such authority—and inmates know this. Instead, the counselor should make sure those requests are communicated to those who can make a commitment, get an answer, and then convey that answer to the groups. In some cases, the person with the authority to make the decision may wish to present that decision in person. This situation should be approached with care to prevent inmates from concluding that they don't have to deal with staff, that they can bypass staff and get higher-ups to intervene.

Shared-interest counseling is one form of application of group counseling. In modified form, it may also be used in cases of individual counseling. An experienced and trusted correctional officer can learn these techniques and apply them in the proper time and setting.

VIII. Closure and Follow-up

The exact time at which the session is to end should be set at the beginning of the session and announced to the group during the counselor's introductory statements. The counselor should notify the group when the session has about five minutes left. Unless there is a special reason for abruptly ending the session, the group should not be surprised by a sudden ending. When terminating the session, the following points should be kept in mind:

1. Give at least five minutes notice before terminating.

2. Be prompt in concluding the session.

3. Summarize the highlights of the session for the group. The summary should include a brief restatement of all points of view expressed by group members; the counselor should be scrupulously fair to all points of view.

4. Call attention to interesting issues that were raised during the session.

5. Suggest the need for further exploration of certain points and issues at subsequent sessions.

6. Underscore and bring to the group's attention any specially related issues that the group might think about or wish to explore at another session.

7. Give special recognition to the group and individual members for participation and for making special contributions or progress. Even minor contributions should receive some recognition.

8. Inform the group when the next session is to be held.

9. If the session has been taped, the group should have had the opportunity during the session to hear the playback. Counselors who would like to play the cassette for other staff should inform the group and ask for permission. Reaffirm that if any member so chooses, the member's statements may be erased from the cassette. Make such erasures in the presence of the group.

The Five-minute Rush

It is common for the group that has been forewarned of the closing time of the session to rush during the last few minutes to offer contributions to the session. Individuals who have kept quiet all along may suddenly speak up. Some who have been resistant for the major portion of the session may suddenly overcome their resistance. Others who have been on the verge of important ideas may suddenly give them expression and tie them up in a succinct package.

The running of the clock creates a sense of urgency. If an individual has been building up toward making a contribution, the impending close of the session heightens the impulse to make the contribution before time runs out.

Group members may want to prolong the session by revealing

The running of the clock creates a sense of urgency.

something earth-shattering. If counselors yield to temptation and prolong the session, they will lessen the chances of this phenomenon occurring at subsequent sessions. If this happens, what is frequently the most productive few minutes in counseling—the last few—will become less productive. The group's sense of urgency to contribute will be dulled.

At the end of the session, the reactions of individual group members are many. These reactions are, at times, quite transparent. At other times, the reactions are so subtle as to be discreet or almost completely internalized. The following are some common reactions:

- a sense of relief that the session has ended
- a sense of fulfillment at having contributed, received, and shared
- an increased sense of self-awareness and an awareness of others
- a sense of having gained acceptance, status, and recognition
- a sense of having participated in an exciting exploration
- a desire to continue with counseling—either in a group or individually
- a denial of any worth to counseling
- an ebb and flow of resistance to counseling
- a desire to escape counseling or some of the inferences of what has occurred or may occur in counseling
- a reappraisal of the counselor by the group
- a reappraisal by the group of itself
- the intensification of the group "we" feeling
- a reappraisal of self
- the beginning of constructive and wholesome forethought
- planning for the future
- an increased sense of accomplishment
- a rush of new ideas and feelings

There are countless reactions. The success of the session can frequently be measured by the degree and intensity of this ferment. Group counseling strives to plant seeds that, with support and reinforcement, may grow in the direction of rehabilitation.

After the Session

A provocative and productive group counseling session tends to build up tremendous momentum. Only naive counselors would assume that just because they have terminated the session, the momentum that propelled the group is dissipated. The momentum continuing past the counseling session is where much of the additional reinforcement of counseling is derived.

When any of the following occur outside counseling sessions, they indicate a strong momentum was built in the session and carried away from it:

1. Group members bring up a subject or issue that was raised in counseling.

2. Group members test some of the things learned in counseling, although in the beginning they may not always correctly and appropriately apply these lessons. At times, in the members' efforts at testing, they can be a trial one moment and highly rewarding the next. Gripes are some of the best indicators of momentum.

3. Group members plan, informally among themselves, what they'll say and do during the next session. This is a process that is important to the development of forethought, planning, and considering consequences.

4. Group members may be exposed to a situation they plan to bring into counseling or vice-versa. Old situations may suddenly be seen in a different light by group members after counseling. They may begin to respond to old situations in a more constructive fashion.

5. The group begins to call itself "we" and to exercise positive group pressure on its members.

6. The group may begin to respond to other people in a more positive fashion and vice-versa.

The counselor, as a member of the group, is also subject to much of the same processes. There will be personal changes, observable and unobservable. Counselors may learn as much about themselves as they learn about the group. They may grow, simultaneously, with the group. When counselors are perceptive enough to observe these processes occurring, the next step is to reinforce them. When they observe that the counseling momentum is continuing, they may encourage group members to do the following:

- test and apply some of the things they've learned in counseling
- plan for subsequent sessions
- further evaluate themselves and their world in light of what they've learned in counseling (the counselor may join the group in this at times)
- further develop the "we" feeling and exert positive pressure from the group on its members
- think about related issues and bring them to the counseling session, so that the members may share in each other's thoughts, plans, discoveries, and ideas
- tie together their total experience acquired in or out of group counseling
- ask for help in particularly difficult areas or for special problems

After the session, or at a later date, the counselor may wish to set up a private conference with a member of the group. This may be done for any number of reasons, but never at cross purposes with the case counselor or caseworker, should one be involved at another level.

A conference may be held at the request of the counselor or the group member. The member may have some problem that he or she could not or would not express in front of the group, but wishes to communicate with the counselor to get help. Or the counselor may notice during the session that the individual is struggling with some special problem that might require individualized services. Such help may come directly from the counselor or through a referral to other staff initiated by the counselor. Other reasons for calling a conference may be that the individual wants some special attention from the counselor or the counselor may wish to personally reinforce special progress the individual has made in group counseling.

Making Referrals

One of the advantages of group counseling is that it works hand-in-glove with individual counseling and aids in increasing the individual's amenability for individual counseling. Counselors are encouraged to use resources whenever the need arises. This process is called referral.

Counselors, for the most part, are capable of working effectively with most problems and situations that arise in counseling. At times, they may need a little help or guidance before approaching and dealing with an issue. Situations will arise that require more special attention and effort than the average counselor may be able to supply. In such cases, the counselor is in a position similar to that of a football quarterback who occasionally has to consult the coach before calling a special play. Once having received advice from the coach, most quarterbacks are able to carry on.

So too, on occasion, the counselor may need advice from a fellow counselor or from other staff. Counselors would be foolish to try to supply services that are beyond their skills, abilities, and responsibilities—especially because counselors have access to people and agencies who are able to secure or supply these specialized services. Such help should be available to counselors as often as needed.

It requires a great deal of maturity and self-discipline to be able to define one's limitations accurately and realistically. Everyone has limitations of some sort in varying degrees. Mature individuals do what they can, and if more assistance is needed, they ask for help. Counselors who need and ask for special help do so not only for themselves, but also for their groups and their members. Counselors are made stronger, not weaker, through the judicious use of resources and the referral process. In deciding when to refer, counselors must determine which approach would be most efficient and effective, considering everything involved.

If counselors determine that they, their group, or any of the group's members need help that they cannot give, they should first consult their supervisor so that the type, quantity, and source of needed help is determined. Counselors and their supervisors then set into motion the process of acquiring this help.

This may involve referral to almost any specialized staff, such as psychiatrists, social workers, psychologists, medical doctors, nurses, court representatives, probation officers, chaplains, administrators, police, legal aid, and so on. A referral can also be made to resource material, such as books, magazines, audiovisual aids, training devices, and programmatic devices.

A directory of social services available in the community is another way of finding and obtaining additional help. If such a directory does not exist, information on these services can be obtained from the local United Way, the yellow pages, state and local government service directories, local professional groups, and many additional sources.

An exceptional source of help may be found in the interdisciplinary team (IDT). Case and group management have become increasingly a shared responsibility. This is true in both community-based and institutional service systems. The IDT shares responsibility for planning, strategizing, and managing cases and groups so that no one person need bear this responsibility alone.

It is customary to assign a caseload to counselors. Under a system that uses an IDT, the counselor is still assigned a caseload but also acts as a hub for the team. This team is composed of representatives from all of the services and disciplines involved with the client/inmate. In an institutional setting, it may include representatives from treatment, education, correctional industries, and custody/security—specifically those who actually deliver these services. The team should include whoever is the "significant other" in the client/inmate's life—a parent, spouse, etc. (However, this individual should not be included in confidential case discussions).

All of these individuals have a stake in management and outcomes. All have a perspective that, at times, may be special and unique. By involving people from different domains and disciplines, a broader perspective is obtained on management, needs, and problem resolution. By joint planning, case and group management affects all the key service and progress areas rather than just some.

However, counselors should not wait until a referral resource is needed. Whenever possible, they should establish and sustain relationships with these resources well ahead of time. This way, if referrals are needed in a time-sensitive situation, various protocols and intake rituals can be avoided.

IX. Evaluating the Session

An evaluation is a form of searching and precise inquiry. The first step in making any evaluation is determining what is being evaluated—what is deemed to be of sufficient importance to warrant special examination and inquiry.

In the evaluation of group counseling, there is an area of examination that is applicable to almost all sessions, counselors, and groups. There are also areas of examination that might be unique to a special counselor, group, or situation. Once counselors sharpen their techniques and abilities of generalized evaluation, they may become increasingly skilled at going from general inquiry to more specific inquiry. In short, once counselors learn what and how to evaluate, their evaluating skills may become sharp and so may their abilities at handling increasingly finer points.

In evaluating the session, counselors should consider the following questions:

1. How closely did content and technique used fulfill the reaching of the following goals of short-term group counseling?

   - create the greatest opportunity for positive growth in the briefest period of time

   - provide opportunities for reeducation

   - support group members' efforts to face and profit from their experiences

   - provide the opportunity for the constructive and channeled venting of excess tension and anxiety

   - provide opportunities to explore and evaluate self and society

   - establish and encourage an atmosphere of self-respect and of mutual respect and acceptance

   - provide the opportunities and the guidance to test what has been learned in group counseling

   - enhance and support all other ongoing programs

2. Were the content and technique of the session the best choice, or would other choices have been more efficient?

3. Were content and technique sufficiently flexible so as to allow changes to be made without interrupting the flow of the session?

4. Were there other choices in content and technique in reserve, if changes had been necessary?

5. If changes were made, what were their effects on the session, the group, and the counselor?

6. Was content and technique based on the needs, interests, motives, and abilities of the group so that a broad range and variety of productive membership participation was made possible and encouraged?

7. Were the presession plans for content and technique realistic in view of what actually happened at the session?

8. Did content and technique encourage the planting of seeds for future sessions?

9. Were the content and technique stimulating?

10. Are the content and technique worth repeating, unmodified, in other sessions? If not, what modifications are indicated? If so, with the same group? Other groups? How often and under what circumstances?

11. Is it possible for other counselors to use this technique and method? If so, what is involved? Is it worth sharing with other counselors?

12. If this method and technique had been used by other counselors in the past, how do these similar applications compare?

13. What are the undesirable facets of using this technique and method? Can these be eliminated? How?

14. How did the method and technique reflect the personality of the counselor? What, if anything, should or could be done about this?

15. Were the content and technique in line with the skills of the counselor?

Besides content and technique, other aspects of counseling should be evaluated. They include (1) group and individual responses, (2) the counselor, (3) the short-term group counseling program itself, and (4) its application to other programs and vice-versa.

Evaluating Group Responses

Counselors wishing to evaluate the responses of their group must first get a clear picture of the make-up of the group and the situations in which and to which the group has been responding. The responses of a group or an individual can be clearly understood only by evaluating the responses in context. Responses taken out of context are subject to misinterpretation. What a person or group does, at any given moment, may be generally applicable to all situations, but the greater possibility is that it is applicable primarily or even solely to the context in which the responses occurred.

This implies that how a group member responded in counseling, of itself, is insufficient evidence to support a belief that these responses are applicable or will be carried over to situations out of counseling. The counselor, in evaluating the group's or the individual's responses, must separate what happened out of counseling. Then, if carry-over of response is evident, the counselor may draw some conclusions about the applicability of a response in counseling to certain situations outside of counseling.

In evaluating the group's responses in counseling, counselors should consider the following:

Degree of participation by group members

1. What is the quality, type, and variety of member participation?

2. What is the quantity and range of participation?

3. What percentage of membership directly participates?

4. During how much of the session did direct group participation lag?

Group expression of motivations, needs, interests, feelings, and suggestions

1. What were they?

2. What did the group do to express them?

3. Were these expressions intense or flat?

4. Did these expressions seem genuine and realistic?

5. What was new, unique, or different about them?

6. How did group expression compare with what the counselor anticipated it would be?

7. Which of these expressions most stimulated the group? How?

8. Which of these expressions flowed freely from the group? How widely were they shared by the group?

9. Which seemed to be most meaningful to the group, according to the group? According to the counselor?

10. Which issue did the group shy away from? How? Were there any observable causes for this? What were they?

11. Was the group fearful, anxious, or tense about any of these expressions? How did they display this?

12. Did the group welcome and accept each member's contributions? Which were especially welcome? Any observable causes for this?

13. Which of these expressions caused the greatest contention? Greatest agreement?

14. What were the significant changes in expression?

Group members' relationships with the counselor

1. What did group members accept about and from the counselor? What did they not accept? How did they express this?

2. In what areas did they seem to trust the counselor?

3. How did they communicate this to the counselor?

4. Was any mistrust resolved to any degree? How?

5. Did group members try to get clues from the counselor about what they thought the counselor "wanted" them to say or do?

6. Did group members mirror the counselor in any way?

7. What did group members seem to expect from the counselor?

8. How did group members react when these expectations were met? How did they react when these expectations were frustrated?

9. Did group members look on the counselor as being a person genuinely interested in helping them? How did they seem to look on the counselor? How did they display this?

10. Were there any detectable and significant changes in group members' attitudes and behavior toward the counselor? What were these changes?

Group receptiveness to short-term group counseling

1. What were the group members' reactions toward the counseling process?

2. How closely did the members' expectations of what counseling would be like parallel the actual session? How did they react to these differences?

3. Did the group see any differences between the atmosphere of counseling and other programs? Did the group act differently in counseling than they did in other programs? How?

4. Did the group plan for future sessions? How?

Relationships within the group

1. Was there any evidence of the beginning of the development or further crystallization of a "we" feeling? How was this demonstrated in the session? Was it positive?

2. Were group reactions indicative of any changes or developments in friendship bonds? What were the antagonisms that appeared?

3. Were the group's leaders, followers, and subgroups in counseling made up of the same people who normally hold these positions? What were any changes? How were these changes made evident?

4. Did the group have enough things in common that they could share? Did they share? How? What?

5. How well were group members able to communicate with each other? How did they communicate?

6. How did the group respond to differences among members?

7. Was the group aware of any positive changes in the inter-relationships? How did they react to this?

8. Did the group relate to the counselor as a group member, "one of us," in the process of identifying themselves as a group?

9. Who were the "outsiders," according to the group, as opposed to whom they thought was "one of us"? Did this waver? How? Under what circumstances?

In evaluating group responses that occur outside of counseling—but related to it—many of the above questions may apply. In some cases, the answers will be identical to those that relate to the in-counseling evaluation. In many cases, the answers will differ and have very different meanings. By comparing and contrasting the group's responses in counseling with those that occur outside of counseling, counselors may further enhance their evaluations of all factors and be better able to appreciate what has really been happening. A better picture of the nature of the counseling processes may thus be obtained.

Evaluating Individual Responses

Counselors should not forget that their group is composed of individuals who are reacting in and to a group situation. The progress of each individual is important. The function of group counseling is to help the individuals who comprise the group. The function of evaluating the responses of individuals is to determine if, how much, and in what way the individual may be helped.

Many of the questions counselors ask in evaluating the group and the sessions may be altered to fit an evaluation of the responses of the individuals. The following are some additional questions:

1. How did this individual's reactions differ from the reaction of other members? How were they the same?

2. What were the individual's special interests, needs, motives, ideas, suggestions, and contributions? How did he or she indicate these? Was he or she anxious to contribute?

3. What were any changes or developments in these?

4. In the reaction of others to the individual, did others accept the individual and his or her contributions? Who were they? What did they accept? What did they reject? What were they passive about?

5. How did the individual react to acceptance? Rejection? Passivity of others? How did the individual react to himself or herself?

6. How did the individual react to the counselor?

7. Did the individual need help? What kind? Was it offered? By whom and how? Was the individual able to use and accept help? Can he or she accept and use more? What kind?

8. Did the individual's interest last all session? Beyond the session into other areas of programming?

9. Was the individual interested, willing, and able to test and apply what was learned in counseling? Were such efforts intensive? Were they appropriate?

10. Does the individual seem interested in participating in future sessions? How does he or she express this?

11. Does the individual express any belief that counseling is helpful to him or her? How?

12. Is the individual concerned about what he or she has done in the past? Is he or she concerned about the future? How? How has counseling helped?

13. Does the individual's presence in counseling carry such weight that the sessions might be appreciably different if he or she were not present? Why? Do others recognize this? Does he or she? How?

14. What were areas, issues, or circumstances in which the individual seemed resistant? Why? How? How were these handled?

Nonverbal responses can reveal a great deal about the individual or the group.

15. What were areas, issues, or circumstances in which the individual reacted openly? Why? How? How were these handled?

Nonverbal Communication as an Evaluation Tool

When considering how people communicate with each other, most think of the verbal methods, that is, the written and spoken word. Counselors depend heavily on verbal communication. Words, written and spoken, are important tools to counselors.

It is important that counselors be skilled in verbal communication—both in sending and receiving. But verbal communication is just one type of communication, and if counselors are insensitive to or unskilled in nonverbal communication, much will escape them. Nonverbal communication is communication between people by a means other than written or spoken words. There are many familiar examples of nonverbal communication. Some of these are as follows:

- facial expressions (smiles, grimaces, etc.)
- postures
- gestures
- body movements
- head shaking and nodding
- yawning
- sleepiness
- laughter
- tears
- perspiration
- blushing
- eye blinking
- teeth gritting
- excessive or impulsive body movement, fidgeting
- wringing hands, hiding hands
- nail biting
- fast, slow, or irregular breathing

There are thousands of examples of nonverbal communication. Most people are sensitive to the more dramatic and openly displayed varieties. Many impressions are gained by having received and reacted to nonverbal communication from others. At times, this form of communication is hardly detectable. The more sensitive counselors are to the reception of this type of communication, the finer their counseling skills may become.

Nonverbal responses can reveal a great deal about the individual or the group. Nonverbal responses may reinforce verbal responses. For example, a person may emphasize an affirmative statement he or she has made by nodding his or her head yes in firm support. In this case, the nonverbal communication lends urgency to the verbal. A person hearing the statement may nod yes, indicating agreement, or no, indicating disagreement. The force and effort expended in such non-verbal communication is frequently a good clue as to strength of the feelings behind it.

There is another aspect involved in interpreting nonverbal communication. This is exemplified by the person who makes a positive and affirmative statement, but then shakes his or her head in such a way as to indicate no or "this is not true" or "I don't agree." Another good illustration of nonverbal communication is the "hard stroll," which many street-wise people affect in their walk and that conveys meaning that they might not dare put into words.

Therefore, the counselor should take into account both the verbal and the nonverbal expressions of the group and its members. An evaluation of just the verbal aspects may be extremely inaccurate, especially because many offenders frequently are skilled in the art of covering up, perhaps more skilled than the counselor is in deciphering. It would take an extraordinary person to be skilled in purposefully covering up nonverbal communication.

Examples of nonverbal communication are called indicators. With patience and practice, counselors can learn to spot these indicators and use them. This skill is applicable both in and out of counseling.

Evaluating the Counselor

Counselors are also subject to evaluation and supervision. The purpose of this procedure is to further develop and train the counselor's skills and to provide a means of exchange of ideas, techniques, methods, information, feelings, and suggestions among staff. The evaluation processes inevitably involve sharing with each other.

Counselors will be evaluating themselves. At times, this will demand that they face themselves and their counseling efforts with courage and conviction enough to tell themselves the truth, as nearly as they can discern it, and as best as they are able. There are few processes that are equal to this in potential for helping counselors attain greater stature as individuals and as professionals. Few beginners can, at first, go through this process efficiently, but this too can be learned. Helping the beginning counselor to learn this is another function of staff who are responsible for the group counseling program.

The following are some appropriate questions counselors may ask when evaluating themselves:

1. How solid were plans for the session, in view of what actually happened during the session?

2. Was what was done in line with the philosophy of the agency and of the group counseling program?

3. How aware am I of my strengths and weaknesses? What are they? What have I done about them? How have these affected the group?

4. What have I done to meet the needs, interests, and abilities of the group and its members?

5. Am I really accepting? Do I feel anxious and tense in a session? Over what? Do I display this to the group? How? What am I doing about it?

6. How fully do I involve the group in my planning?

7. Have I shared my experiences with others? What am I most reluctant to share with others? Are they able to share with me? Do I feel free to ask for help from others?

8. Are there certain types of people, statements, and actions toward or against which I am biased? Which? What do I do about it?

9. Am I comfortable when people confide in me? What confidences am I most tempted to divulge?

10. Have my experiences as a counselor changed me? In what way am I different? What have I learned?

11. How do I feel about these experiences?

12. How have I reacted to pressures coming from the group? Its members? Others? Self? Which pressures don't annoy me at all? Least? Most? What am I doing about dealing more effectively with these pressures?

13. What, in these experiences, has been most rewarding to me? What has most disappointed me?

14. Do I feel willing and able to continue with counseling groups? Why?

15. Have I applied what I've learned in counseling? To subsequent sessions? To my general dealings with the group? To others? To myself? How? With what results?

Using Evaluations

Once counselors have evaluated these aspects for themselves, what next? How may the evaluations be used so the group counseling program is strengthened? This is a multistep procedure.

1. The counselor holds the session.

2. The counselor evaluates the session, group and individual responses, and himself or herself.

3. The counselor shares these evaluations with fellow counselors and other staff who, in turn, share with the counselor their observances, experiences, ideas, suggestions, and technical knowledge. This is a refining process analogous to the refining of crude oil into many specialized products.

4. The sharing process becomes, at the same time, a learning, training, planning, and growth process.

5. The counselor, after participating in the refinement processes, applies the products of these processes to himself or herself, his or her group and individual group members, his or her techniques and methods, his or her plans for subsequent sessions, and other related programs.

6. The counselor initiates the next session, and the cycle starts again.

7. With successive cycles, short-term group counseling may become a progressively more efficient adjustment and rehabilitative tool.

This book is not the final word. The opportunity to make a creative contribution to one's profession comes too infrequently to be ignored. Most of those in corrections chose their profession because they believe that they would be fulfilling themselves as human beings who not only wish to serve but who also wish to serve creatively. This is both the challenge and the opportunity of this program. This book and the short-term group counseling program have been created in an effort to add more tools to corrections' professional arsenal. It remains for interested corrections professionals to improve this and themselves.

Reference

Kubler-Ross, Elizabeth. 1981. *Living With Death and Dying*. New York: MacMillan Publishing Company, Inc.

Suggested Readings

Benjamin, A. 1981. *The helping interview*. Boston: Houghton Mifflin.

Berg, R. C., and G. L. Landreth. 1990. *Group counseling: Concepts and procedures*. Muncie, Ind.: Accelerated Development.

Corey, S. M. 1963. *Helping other people change*. Columbus, Ohio: Ohio State University Press.

Davis, L. E., and E. N. Proctor. 1989. *Race, gender and class: Guidelines for practice with individuals, families, and groups*. Englewood Cliffs, N.J.: Prentice Hall.

Dwyer, W., and J. Friend. 1977. *Counseling techniques that work: Applications to individual and group counseling*. New York: Sovereign Books.

Freedman, J. L. 1975. *Crowding and behavior*. New York: Viking Press.

Gazda, G. M. 1989. *Group counseling: A developmental approach*. Boston: Allyn and Bacon.

George, R. L. 1990. *Counseling the chemically dependent: Theory and practice*. Englewood Cliffs, N.J.: Prentice Hall.

George, R. L., and D. Dustin. 1988. *Group counseling: Theory and practice*. Englewood Cliffs, N.J.: Prentice Hall.

Kemp, C. G. 1970. *Foundations for group counseling*. New York: McGraw-Hill.

Knowles, J. W. 1964. *Group counseling*. Englewood Cliffs, N.J.: Prentice Hall.

May, R. 1989. *The art of counseling*. New York: Gardner Press.

McCarthy, G., K. Merriam, and S. Coffman. 1984. *Taking it out: A guide to groups for abused women*. Seattle, Wash.: Seal Press.

Ohlsen, M. M., A. Horne, and C. F. Law. 1988. *Group counseling*. New York: Holt, Rinehart and Winston.

Perez, J. F. 1985. *Counseling the alcoholic*. Muncie, Ind.: Accelerated Development.

Perez, J. F. 1986. *Counseling the alcoholic group*. New York: Gardner Press.

Powell, T. J., and S. J. Enright. 1990. *Anxiety and stress management*. New York: Routledge.

Rogers, R., and C. S. McMillin. 1988. *Don't help: A positive guide to working with the alcoholic*. New York: Bantam Books.

Trotzer, J. P. 1989. *The counselor and the group: Integrating theory, training and practice*. Muncie, Ind.: Accelerated Development.

Weissberg, M. P. 1983. *Dangerous secrets: Maladaptive responses to stress*. New York: W.W. Norton.

Willis, J. T. 1990. *Implications for effective psychotherapy with African-American families and individuals*. Matteson, Ill.: Genesis Publications.

About the Author

Ellis S. Grayson's career includes working with class I street gangs, those who have killed and retain the potential for doing so again. He has worked at the level of line staff and executive in both adult and juvenile correctional facilities as well as with alternatives to incarceration. He directed Pennsylvania's first state-operated diagnostic and classification center for juvenile offenders. He also served as an executive with Pennsylvania's Bureau of Correction.

As a young professional, he worked at Philadelphia's Youth Study Center, a detention facility for juvenile offenders awaiting the court's disposition. It was there, in 1957, that he developed a model for short-term group counseling. That model became a template duplicated nationally and internationally.

Grayson has authored more than three dozen books and professional articles. He is currently writing a book on the elements of one-on-one counseling.

Grayson is currently a staff trainer, specializing in group and case counseling. He also consults on the design of new staff development and in-service training curricula for state correctional systems.